HAGANAH Ship
EXODUS 1947

ISRAEL: IMAGES & IDEAS

Presented to
Mr. and Mrs. James Greenbaum
Leaders Circle Co-Chairs 1989
With appreciation
Jewish Federation
Palm Springs Desert Area
April 12, 1989

# ISRAEL:

# IMAGES & IDEAS

VIEWFINDER PUBLICATIONS  OLD CHATHAM, NY 12136

*OVERLEAF: Saturday night celebration at Kibbutz Nasholim.*
*ENDLEAVES: Overloaded with European refugees, the Haganah*
*ship "Exodus 1947" arrives in Haifa Harbor on July 18, 1947. The*
*immigrants were forcibly returned to Europe.*

Copyright © 1988 by: Viewfinder Publications, Inc.
& Timothy Nichols

Viewfinder Publications, Inc.
P.O. Box 41
Old Chatham, NY 12136

ISBN: 0-942529-02-2

Library of Congress Card Catalog No. 88-051218

Viewfinder books are available at special discounts for bulk purchases
for sales promotions, premiums, fund-raising or educational use.
For details, contact:

Viewfinder Publications, Inc.
P.O. Box 41
Old Chatham, NY 12136
(518) 794-7767 or 9767

10  9  8  7  6  5  4  3  2  1

Publisher: Clay Hutchison

Managing Editor: Elizabeth Martin

Photographic Editor: Bryan Cheney

Contributing Photographers: Ronen Amit (Tel Aviv), Dee Dauphinee,
Itamar Grinberg (Eilat), David Haas, Yakis Kidron (Tev Aviv), Yair Nahor
(Haifa), Keren Or Agency (Haifa), Richard Riddell, Paul Souders, Bali
Szabo, Clifton York.

Design & Graphics:   Timothy Nichols, with Amanda Veal
NPS of Vermont, Inc.,
P.O. Box 258
Jamaica, VT 05343
(802) 874-4395 / 4915

Printed and bound in Italy by New Interlitho, SpA, Milan.

# CONTENTS

# WITH SPECIAL THANKS:

Yaacov Amit
David Angel
Prof. Amram Ashri
Barri Avnerre
Daphna Barak
Shulamit Ben-Dor
Prof. Louis Berkofsky
J. Blaustein Inst. for Desert Research
Ra'anan Boral
Amir Cheshin
Daliya Dromi
Rina Feldman
Rabbi Menachem Fruman
Uzia Galil
Micha Gidron
Nathan Goldblum, MD
Hebrew University
Rafi Horowitz
Eli Hurvitz
Bishop Guregh Kapikian
Prof. Alex Keynan
Eli Kubesi
Prof. Amia Lieblich

Prof. Moshe Lissak
Prof. Benjamin Mazar
Sevanah Meryn
Benny Meushkin
Isaac Meyer
Nachemia Meyers
Esther Nehab
Rabbi Meir Porush
Kurt Raveh
Prof. Amos Richmond
Dan Seusskind
Moshe Shackak
Meira Shacham
Binyamin Shafrir
Prof. Lawrence Stager
Prof. Gerald Steinberg
Prof. William Taub
The Technion
Prof. Yoash Vaadia
Weizmann Institute
Gen. Ezer Weizman

EL AL Israel Airlines

6

"DEALISM IS IN DIRECT PROPORTION TO THE DIS-
tance from the problem," said Israeli press liaison
Rafi Horowitz, in defense of American criticism
of Israel's handling of the Palestinian problem.
It's a profound thought, one that has more
relevance to Israel than meets the eye — or
rather the ear. Paradoxically Israel is just distant
enough to keep its affairs something of a mystery, yet
close enough in the hearts of the Diaspora to retain an
image that is often just that — an image. There's the
rub, because that image equates loyalty to Israel with
approval of everything her government does.

In a land where a new political party or movement
can spring up like a weed, diversity of thought is
acknowledged by all. But in the Diaspora, where the
undeniably heroic image of Israel endures — also like
a weed — departure from the government mainstream
never fails to push the limits of toleration.

Last March some 30 US Senators wrote an open let-
ter to Prime Minister Yitzhak Shamir, urging him
to settle the Palestinian problem by making territorial
concessions if necessary. Their appeal fell on deaf ears,
and many Israelis were indignant at what they felt was
outside interference. This fall several of these same
senators are campaigning for re-election, yet even
those five who are Jews have met stiff resistance from
Jewish constituents, confirming once again that outside criticism of Israeli policy is tantamount to treason.

The lesson in all this is that only Israelis have
unrestricted license to pass critical comment on their
country, a fact not lost on the Editors of *Israel: Images
& Ideas*. Accordingly they made the decision to have
Israelis do the work for them. Israelis themselves would
provide the outspoken color only they could deliver,
taking the responsibility for it only they could shoulder.

From February through June few efforts were spared
to collect as wide a sampling of Israeli society as possible. Photographically, the Editors sought to capture a
slice of the real Israel at 40, to look "beyond the Wall,"
if you will, at truly representative facets of the country. In so doing a conscious effort was made to avoid

the sensational and seek the unusual.

Meanwhile the thrust of the text would evolve from
interviews with a collage of professors and politicians,
holy men and common men to provide a diverse but
nevertheless homegrown window into Israel's 40th
year across a five-month time frame.

But as events would prove, this would not be just *any*
five-month period. As preparations for celebrating
Israel's 40th anniversary consumed the attention of
Jewish communities at home and abroad, the Palestinian uprising was approaching its zenith — and consuming the attention of the world's newsmedia. Daily
television broadcasts sensationalized the *intifada* and
excoriated Israel's police and army reaction to
countless strikes, stonings, tire burnings and petrol
bombings. Night after night a beleaguered Defense
Minister Yitzhak Rabin appeared on Western television, fruitlessly trying to explain his policies to a suddenly hostile world more anxious to find villains and
victims than practical solutions.

Somehow it wasn't fair. After 40 years of struggling
independence, Israel's very integrity was jeopardized; David had been transformed into Goliath simply
because he had tried ensure his own survival. Worst
of all, the battle lines were forming on the home front
as issues polarized the people as never before. From
all corners of the political spectrum individuals step-
ped forward to identify the problems. They had met the
"enemy," and it was the Arabs, it was the PLO, it was
the Gush Emunim, it was the Peace Now movement,
it was...it was...the Israelis themselves.

The fight was on; Israeli vs. Arab, Orthodox vs.
secular, retain territory for geographical security, give
it up for political security. Old issues. New issues. All
issues. What a hell of a time to do a book on Israel...

But what a wonderful moment to capture a people's
real motivations, exposed by light that only an emergency can provide. What a chance to gather unalloyed
private opinions on sensitive issues. What a challenge
to photograph Israel *not* as a travelogue, but as an exceptional place of exceptional accomplishment. ∎

I hope that one day I will come to the States and I will see the TV showing the exact borders of Israel. Every time I was in the States and saw a news program about Israel and the Arab countries, they always showed Israel close up on the map with only little pieces of the Arab countries — with Israel always in the center. They never show that Israel is only a pinpoint on the map with very large Arab countries all around."

ELI KUBESI, THE JEWISH AGENCY

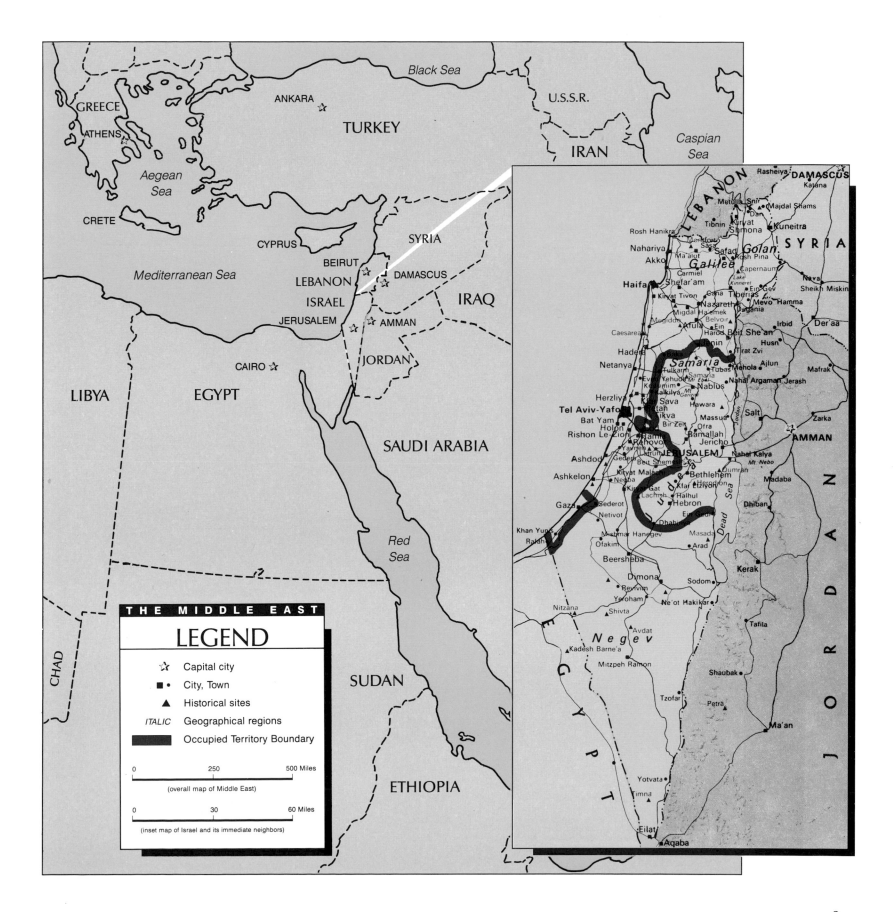

Black Sea

GREECE
ANKARA ☆
ATHENS ☆
TURKEY
U.S.S.R.

Aegean
Sea

IRAN

Caspian
Sea

CRETE

CYPRUS

SYRIA

Mediterranean Sea

BEIRUT ☆
LEBANON
DAMASCUS ☆

ISRAEL

IRAQ

JERUSALEM ☆

AMMAN ☆

JORDAN

LIBYA

EGYPT

CAIRO ☆

SAUDI ARABIA

Red
Sea

CHAD

**THE MIDDLE EAST**

# LEGEND

☆  Capital city

■  City, Town

▲  Historical sites

*ITALIC*  Geographical regions

█  Occupied Territory Boundary

0        250        500 Miles

(overall map of Middle East)

0        30        60 Miles

(inset map of Israel and its immediate neighbors)

SUDAN

ETHIOPIA

DAMASCUS
LEBANON
Rasheiya
Katana

Metulla Snir
Tibnin Dan Majdal Shams
Kiryat Shmona Kuneitra

Rosh Hanikra
Nahariya Meron Sasa Safad Golan SYRIA
Akko Ma'alot Rosh Pina
Carmiel Capernaum
Haifa Shefar'am Lake Naua
Kiryat Tivon Cana Kinneret Ein Gev Sheikh Miskin
Nazareth Tiberias Mevo Hamma
Migdal Ha-emek Degania
Caesarea Afula Belvoir
Harod Beit She'an Irbid Der'aa
Hadera Jenin Husn
Netanya Samaria Tubas Mahola Ajlun
Tulkarm Mt Ebal Nahal Argaman Jerash Mafrak
Even Yehuda Samaria Nablus
Kedumim Mt Gerizim
Herzliya Kalkilya Hawara Salt
Tel Aviv-Yafo Kfar Sava Massua
Petah Tikva Ofra Zarka
Bat Yam Bir Zeit Jericho
Holon Ofra AMMAN
Rishon Le-Zion Ramallah Nahal Kalya
Rehovot Latrun JERUSALEM Mt Nebo
Ashdod Yavne Gedera Bethlehem Qumran
Beit Shemesh Madaba
Ashkelon Kiryat Malachi Kfar Etzion
Negba Dhiban
Kiryat Gat Halhul Dead Sea
Gaza Sederot Lachish Hebron
Khan Yunis Netivot Ein Gedi
Rafah Mishmar Hanegev Masada
Ofakim Arad Kerak
Beersheba
Dimona Sodom
Reuvim
Yeroham Ne'ot Hakikar
Nitzana Tafila
Shivta
Avdat
*Negev*
Kadesh Barne'a
Mitzpeh Ramon Shaubak

Tzofar Petra

Ma'an

Yotvata
Timna

Eilat
Aqaba

EGYPT

JORDAN

9

*Holding aloft the Torah; Passover celebration at the Western Wall.*

*A Haredi on Mea She'arim Street, Jerusalem.*

*Sunset in the Negev Desert.*

*The Monastery of the Temptation in Wadi Tasun, near Jericho.*

*Modern glass production at the Haifa Technion.*

*The Mosque of Ahmed Jezzar in Acco, built in 1781.*

ABOVE: Aluf (Major General) Ezer Weizman
in the cockpit of his black Spitfire; and as
Commander of the IAF with Prime Minister
David Ben-Gurion and Defense Minister
Shimon Peres upon the arrival of Israel's first
French jet trainer, a Fouga Magister.
RIGHT: Minister Without Portfolio Ezer
Weizman on Israel's 40th Anniversary of
Independence, May 15, 1988.

# FOREWORD

EZER WEIZMAN

ANYONE WHO PREFERS TO SEE ISRAEL today the same as the Zionist founders perceived it forty years ago simply does not accept changing world and local situations. The Israel that my late uncle Chaim envisaged is totally different from the country which I've seen develop. After all, there are 50 years between us. He was born in 1874; I was born in 1924. The world is no longer the same world; relationships between countries are not the same. Look, for example, at what became of Japan and Germany in the 40 years since the Second World War. Look at China in the last forty years. Mao Zedung would get out of his grave now if he could see the things going on with Gorbachev!

I was born into the British Empire. I served His Majesty as a Palestinian; I walked around with "Palestine" on the shoulder patch of my RAF uniform. Today "Palestinian" means something negative — I don't think so myself — but to the majority of people it does.

Who ever dreamt in my lifetime that the England of my childhood would turn into the England of today? When I left Bombay aboard a British troopship in February 1946, it was the beginning of a completely new world, although nobody realized at the time just how much it would change. I always tease British friends of mine that I took part in switching off the lights in the British Empire!

Nearly a hundred years ago people first thought of political Zionism. Zionism has been a Jewish tradition ever since we left here 2000 years ago; we all prayed for "Next year in Jerusalem." Now think of going back to the land of our ancestors a hundred years ago, faced with the task of changing the way of life of the Jew then known to the world. This was a Jew who was somewhat different in his community, had a different religion, sometimes spoke a different language, was not like the rest.

Uncle Chaim's idea was to create a different life for the Jew, and therefore a different character for the Jewish people. For example, when people emigrated 200 years ago to America it was that very process which made them Americans. Now there was no longer just the Dutch boy, the German boy or the Italian boy; there was the *American* boy. They went there to live a different life, and their new environment created America and Americanism. Now a hundred years ago, the Zionists had a very similar aim: to create a different sort of Jew, an Israeli.

For example, in earlier times you never heard much of Jewish fighter pilots, tank commanders or important generals. You had an odd one here and there in the world wars, and these fellows were usually pointed out by the press as the exceptions. These days it's common knowledge that some of the best fighter pilots in the world are Israelis. Now I won't say it was the aim of my late uncle to be a fighter pilot or create a society of soldiers, although his son Michael, my cousin, was lost in the RAF in 1941.

Zionism has been a revolution in Jewish life. Jews made aliyah not simply because they longed for a better economic life, but for something very much deeper in this case — to recreate the land of the Jews. But remember, it's much easier to create a revolution than to mold and consolidate its fruits. Here we wanted to create a nation that would feel secure physically, secure economically and secure traditionally. We wanted the country to be attractive for Jews to immigrate. If we are only 3½ million here, when the free world today has probably 8 million Jews — excluding Russia — then something is not yet attractive enough in Israel. We should have had at least double that here by now.

America had her revolution when the British were smartly asked to leave. Then for a long time the country had its upheavals, like the Civil War. Russia had her revolution; Gorbachev is still consolidating that after so many years. France, too, had a revolution and then years of upheavals in its aftermath. I only hope that Israel won't suffer something similar.

It's very easy to change something drastically. It's like a battle, a defined action, where the most interesting part comes *after* the battle. Following the defeat of Japan, a sensible world decided to help rebuild the country — with checks and balances, of course. The ironic thing was that the rebuilding process was led by General MacArthur, the man who played the foremost role in her defeat. And the idea for rebuilding Germany and Europe came from another military man, US Chief-of-Staff General Marshall.

So the aftermath of a crisis is the most important part of the battle; and in Israel we're still living the long, slow process of consolidating the fruits of our revolution. We just can't pat ourselves on the belly and say "Ah ha! We've done a great job over these 40 years." Yes, we've done many good things; we've also done a few wrong things. We didn't succeed everywhere we wanted.

**W**hen we decided to go back to the land, we had to create industry, we had to re-create the Hebrew language, we had to start our own academies. I don't think my grandmother, born something like 130 years ago, ever thought that her grandchildren would go to a Hebrew school or university. That old girl, the mother of Chaim Weitzmann, was a great lady. She died in 1939 after bringing to life 12 children. If you had told her 100 years ago that her grandson, yours truly, would study in Hebrew — that's a hell of a revolution!

Ever since the first settlements started about 100 years ago, in places like Petach Tikva and Rishon Lezion, the main things we confronted after malaria and tilling the land were the Arabs. This was a most important factor, because unfortunately they defied us and fortunately they molded us — in a way. But as for continuing that molding process today, enough's enough.

Before 1948 we had defense forces primarily to protect ourselves from the Arabs. Later on there was a short period of blowing hell out of the British (I don't think there's any respectable nation in the world that didn't fight the British at one time or another), but our underground defense groups were raised principally to defend ourselves from marauding Arabs. We grew up in a cowboys-and-Indians atmosphere.

To be objective, I don't know how I would have acted had I been an Arab during that period, confronted by a bunch of Europeans who bought land and started creating new villages. These newcomers were also of a different religion. Now Islam and Judaism are very close to each other; Arabic and Hebrew are cousins, but from the word go, troubles began. There were big riots in 1921, 1929, and then 1936.

**T**he first real crisis between the Arab nations and us came in 1948; until then we fought only local Arabs. It will be 40 years now, on the 29th of May, that I first struck an Egyptian column just south of Tel Aviv. We went up in four Messerschmitts; my wingman was killed that day. Another was killed later on.

When '48 came, Iraq, Saudi Arabia, Syria, Egypt, Jordan, Lebanon — the whole lot attacked us. It was a hell of a fight; we lost 6,000 killed, one percent of the population. For comparison's sake, God forbid in 18 months that America should lose 2½ million men. War is usually the sum total of the stupidity of human beings, but usually you come to terms with your enemies after each one. Unfortunately we did not.

The War of Independence was the first real military campaign between the Arabs and us. It frustrated them and took away their will to negotiate. But for us, it made us nine feet tall. Well, there's a limit to how tall you can be, and also a limit to how low you can bend. In '48 the Arabs excused themselves because they said they had rotten governments. Probably they were right. They had King Farouk, King Feisal, King Abdullah; shortly thereafter they had their own revolutions. For the next several years we had little skirmishes on the way to the '56 War in Sinai. Then the Arabs said "Ha! You Israelis won because you went in with the French and the British" — which was true. Then came the Six Day War in '67 and for once they couldn't say a word about their defeat. In '67, by the way, we had not a single American combat plane — only French ones. We had some 200 fighter planes, plus about 25 small trainers, but we blew hell out of them before they woke up. In six days we shot up around 520 planes, in the air, on the ground. The Egyptian air force was taken out in three to four hours. Motty Hod was in command at the time, but that operation was the work of quite a team, training for years before. You don't prepare for a war like this with a snap of your fingers.

Today everybody talks about how great the air force is. Believe me, 21 years ago, on the eve of the Six Day War, not many believed in what we said we could do. In those days we were the lightweights of the armed forces, not like the tough infantrymen. We flyers were the "Brylcreem Boys," as we used to be called in England in the old days. Up again, down again, a hot shower and a good meal. Nowadays everybody points out the contributions of the air force to Israeli defense, to Israeli technology.

After the Six Day War came the War of Attrition with the Arabs, and then followed the Yom Kippur War in 1973. 25 years after Independence came this most important war, and it was the first time the Egyptians could say they gave the Israelis a bloody nose.

Egyptian President Anwar Sadat apparently felt he needed this war, as he would later tell me time and time again. Sadat used say that after the October War he could speak to me with a clean conscience. Now that "clean conscience" was not meant for me but for his own people. The fact is that the status quo of 1967-73 was broken by the October War.

Sadat then came to the conclusion that there need be no more war, that it was now time to talk peace. Quite rightly, from the Egyptian point of view, and because his country had such phenomenal internal problems, he decided to make peace with Israel. It would open the road to America, and the United States would help him.

I think Sadat was a great man, and one of the most interesting personalities I've met in my life. Later we actually became quite close, as close as people like us can be close, and when he was assassinated it was a great personal loss for me and a great loss to the Middle East as a whole.

At this point we come to nowadays. After 40 years of sovereignty, we have now had a relationship with Egypt for over ten years. That's a hell of a long time. And likewise we have to reflect upon what we have done in those ten years to cope with the Arab problem.

Now what did we agree to at the Camp David peace talks? When Sadat arrived here in 1977, he said, "Look, I'll make peace with you, and you'll give me back the Sinai." We dilly-dallied about the Sinai, but the fact is we gave it back. People forget how deep the problems were then; it took 16 long months from Sadat's arrival here in Jerusalem to the signing of the treaty after Camp David.

From the beginning our biggest problem has been how to come to an understanding with the Arab world. All generations of Israelis, from right to left, from Jabotinsky to Weizmann, wanted accommodation with the Arabs. They all felt this need for security, which is also the current basis for our lack of progress in coming together with the Arabs.

Our next problem was what to do about the Palestinians. Now let's see what Menachem Begin finally did. With all due respect to government colleagues in different parties, I left the government in 1980 because I felt they didn't adhere to what Begin had signed. Camp David talks about comprehensive and durable peace with Egypt, but the main issue is that it refers to the Palestinian people, to the necessity of solving their problem in all its aspects, enabling them to determine their own future. The final status of the West Bank and Gaza would then be determined in negotiations between the Jordanian and Palestinian delegations.

After a period of autonomy of between three to five years — autonomy is not a permanent solution but an interim arrangement — there is to be a solution that is not defined at Camp David but is agreed upon by all sides to be discussed later on.

So what will be the final status of the West Bank and Gaza? This disposition is based on UN Resolution 242, which discusses the territories taken in the '67 War; it does not talk about all the territories in general. The formula for future agreement on territories was what Begin signed for.

So we signed at Camp David, with Sadat hoping that the Palestinian problem would be solved; and we fulfilled the bilateral agreement on Sinai. The fact is that we're now back to the international borders, and diplomatically an Israeli flag flies in Egypt, an Egyptian flag flies in Tel Aviv. It's a coldish peace, not as good as it should have been, and for one big reason: the Palestinian problem.

Now, unfortunately, some political forces don't want to talk about giving back an inch of the West Bank or Gaza, although no Likud government has annexed the West Bank and Gaza in 21 years. That would be contrary to what Begin signed. I claim that Begin regretted what he'd signed, therefore among other things, that's why he resigned.

I left Begin's government in May of 1980 because I thought that the Palestinian problem — addressed by the signature of an Israeli Prime Minister, an Egyptian President, countersigned by a President of the United States — was not dealt with as it should have been. I'm being mild because today is the 40th Anniversary, and I don't want to get into political strife.

It took 10 years after the arrival of Sadat for upheavals to begin on the West Bank and Gaza. The Palestinians said that the Arab world didn't solve their problems, that the Israelis got their Egyptian compact on Sinai but then stopped looking for further solutions.

And now we've reached a situation of hours, days and months of fragile truce. After 40 years of sovereignty, and 100 years of practical Zionism, are we going to give up part of the West Bank, all the West Bank, part of Gaza, all of Gaza? Or are we going to stick to ideas that should be changed?

Here there are three vital things to consider: our defense, who our friends are, and what sort of armed forces we need. Let me begin with defense. To the best of my analysis, to secure a defense in modern times, especially in a changed world, the number one ingredient is an understanding with your neighbors. In other words, peace.

When I was Defense Minister I was often attacked for dealing so much with peace. My favorite answer was that nothing contributes to defense more than peace, which has to be guarded constantly. So despite the fact that our peace with Egypt isn't as it should be, today Israel has more defense than we ever had before. We have to look after it properly; just like a plant.

The second thing is world support. As I noted before, we fought the 1967 War without a single American plane; now we fly the latest in American equipment. On the ground, all our tanks now have American engines. So one great ingredient of defense is whether or not you have a superpower with you. As for America, with all due respect for some of my colleagues who say that we're a strategic asset to the United States, I think that the United States is a hell of a strategic asset to *us*! And $1.8 billion annually for defense is not small fry.

Then last, but not least, is what sort of armed forces we need. Right now we have the strongest military we've ever had, although you've still to meet the general who'll tell you he's got enough. There are two kinds kinds of generals who write books. The first is the one who'll tell you how he won the war without enough equipment, and the other who justifies that he lost the war because he didn't have enough. Notice how proudly I noted we had only 200 fighters back in '67. If something had gone wrong in '67, as it did in '73, most of the excuses would have been technical excuses.

When I look back at the air force I commanded and the air force General Bednun commands now, boy, is he lucky! He's got a beauty; and he looks after it very well. The army and the navy are also outstanding. We've never had America with us as we have now. Russia, perhaps, is also changing, I hope. We have the beginnings of a peace with Egypt. So what the hell am I afraid of?

It's the time to look for markets, not for wars. There's another ingredient for defense. When you have peace with your neighbors, should you not also come to close economic relations? I believe we should consider our commercial possibilities in the Middle East.

Now is the time to decide a course of action. If we give up part of the West Bank and the whole of Gaza, will it be detrimental to our defense? I think not — depending on the agreements. For instance, we have an open agreement with Egypt; Sinai is not a demilitarized zone, but only thin forces are there. So why can't we have such an agreement with the West Bank and Gaza? Again, what the hell am I afraid of?

From an historical point of view, however, the discussion is completely different. If you want to go by the Bible, then you can cross borders all over the Middle East. Where was the Kingdom of David? Where was the Kingdom of Solomon? Where was this and where was that? When David escaped the anger of King Saul, he fled to the Gaza Strip. If you read your Bible, you'll see he went to the Philistines. Then you can read that we were on the Euphrates, etcetera. History and going by the Bible are important, but securing peace is far more important. So as a politician, I'm willing to give up the whole Gaza Strip and parts of the West Bank.

N ow the question is whom do I talk to? I will talk to anyone who demonstrates he has the authority to conclude a deal with me, can guarantee a ceasefire, recognizes the State of Israel, and is willing to talk to me on 242 — nothing else. I say openly that even if Arafat comes in with these four ingredients and proves that he has them, I'll talk to him as well.

Above all, he must have the authority to effect a cease-fire, as Sadat did by simply concluding there would be no more war. Or as, without talking peace, the Syrians under Hafez Assad have done on the Golan Heights, where there has been no trouble for 14½ years. We can't go back to the 1948 borders, but we must go *somewhere*.

So I'll deal with whoever has the authority. One is Assad, one is Hussein, one is Mubarak — who incidentally is doing a great job in a country with very serious problems. One of the greatest things Sadat did in his lifetime was to appoint Mubarak as his deputy. He couldn't have chosen anyone better. The proof of the pudding is in the eating — the way he runs Egypt with its tremendous difficulties. His country has terrific population problems. With a rise of about 1.1 million per year, by the year 2000 Egypt will have a population of more than 100 million! So Hosni Mubarak has turned out to be a very underrated person, much like Truman; perhaps even greater.

One thing seems almost sure. Whatever is decided on the West Bank and Gaza to resolve the Palestinian problem, Jordan will be dragged in and eventually return to Camp David as a Jordanian-Palestinian delegation. The sooner we get to this and consolidate the peace we started with Egypt, define our life with the Arabs differently, and start looking at them through joint enterprises and mutual respect, Israel will flourish, the area will flourish. Israel will then be a country with open doors to Cairo, to Damascus, to Amman, to Baghdad, to Beirut. Instead of Israelis looking for markets only in France, England and America, there will be new markets developed here in the Middle East. Then, perhaps for the first time in a long while, Israel will be more attractive to immigrant Jews. And the sooner the better.

In recent months we've heard so much in the media about what happened 40 years ago. Now I'm much more concerned with what's going to happen in the next few months. It's all very nice to talk about the past, and progress since then has been very great indeed. But anyone who goes too deep into the past — especially the recent past like this — can have the tendency to neglect the future.

Jerusalem
15. 5. 1988

*Cutting down papyrus in preparation for draining swamps north of Lake Kinneret. Kibbutz Amir, June 1940.*

# INTRODUCTION

**D**O YOU KNOW THE TOWN OF SAFED? IT'S about 13,000 people in the northern Galilee. Just a short trip west off the main road north to Kiryat Shmona. No? How about the city of Zefat, an ancient center of Jewish mysticism and also in the northern Galilee? Maybe? Have you ever heard of Sfat, with its colorfully decorated artists' colony built along old winding streets? Yes, that's the one; just north of Lake Kinneret.

Of course all three are one and the same town, despite the bewildering variety of spellings not always engendered by transliteration. It's just like Israel: all different, all the same. One man's Safed is another's Zefat. One man's Israel is courageous, totally demoratic; another's is loutish, bureaucratically stifling. During the five month span that staffers and editors of *Israel: Images & Ideas* spent in Israel, Eretz Yisrael revealed itself to be all of the above. And more.

*Israel: Images & Ideas* is a reflection of Israel in 1988, as seen by an international group of journalists and photographers. It's an overview of Israeli successes of the past and present, from the frontier agriculture of the Ashkenazi Labour Zionists to the multi-racial, technological society whose standard of education is the envy of the Middle East — and beyond. Most of all, it's a five-month window into contemporary Israel around the period of its 40th Anniversary.

But while Israel celebrated, the five month-old Palestinian uprising, or *intifada*, was consuming a much larger share of the media attention, catalyzing and polarizing Israeli public opinion like never before. Fire bombings and stonings were met by rubber bullets and beatings from the army and police. Quickly, very quickly Western media forgot about the 40th, and their nightly broadcasts focused on beleaguered Defense Minister Yitzhak Rabin trying to keep order in the occupied territories while not appearing too heavy-handed. It was a losing effort.

The floodgates of public opinion burst when CBS aired a segment showing four Israeli soldiers beating a young Palestinian with truncheons. Like a Wall Street panic, public opinion turned on Israel. Newspaper editorials excoriated the government and its 19 years of doing little about the political rights of 1.5 million Palestinians living under military law in Gaza and the West Bank. Almost overnight this most modern and enlightened country was cast in the outlaw's role, as world media focused with a vengeance on the intifada.

At once, in Israel and the Diaspora alike, Jews rallied to support the State. Some were extremely outspoken in demonstrating their unalloyed praise for the government and its policies; others were more equivocal, careful to separate their love for the Jewish State from their strong disapproval of its Palestinian policies.

Despite the hoopla generated at home and in the Diaspora, it came to matter comparatively little that Israel's 40th birthday was fast approaching. The Yishuv's biggest problem had already endured a hundred birthdays and was still front page news: the Arabs. Suddenly politicians were more frenzied, people more frustrated. While Jewish leaders in the Diaspora had some success in persuading their flocks into universally espousing an "Israel right or wrong we love you" posture, leaders in Israel had no such luck. The strains of the Unity government were never more apparent than when Prime Minister Yitzhak Shamir (Herut Party) was turning a deaf ear to US Secretary of State George Schultz, while Foreign Minister Shimon Peres (Labour Party) was tentatively extending a hand to the Palestinians.

**A**gainst that political backdrop, the Editors spent February through June collecting their material. Photographically, the Editors' challenge was to produce something unusual — but not too unusual. Early-on it was decided to avoid the sensational and the hackneyed, and to seek out a measure of the unusual wherever possible. Not that a kibbutz, the Negev, the Golan, an army patrol are at all unusual, but they're generally off the beaten path for the average tourist coffee table book.

Benny Meushkin, Director of Public Relations at Hebrew University, selected a group of authoritative faculty to interview in Jerusalem, while other staffers circulated throughout the country to record people big and small as they commented on and complained about current issues. And because Israel is a world technological leader, strong representatives from those industries were contacted, notably Uzia Galil, founder and CEO of Elron Electronics and head of the Technion Board of Governors.

For Israel it might have been the worst of times. For writers it was the best of times to gather interviews, and indeed that's how this book took the shape it did. It may be a product of a Diaspora group, but its outlooks and opinions are as homegrown as tomorrow morning's *Jerusalem Post*. If they are not always correct on an individual basis, at least Israelis have a right to their own opinions, and the old adage "two Israelis, three opinions" has never been more true than in the bitter days of the 1988 intifada.

L eviticus 19:34 instructs us "If a stranger lives with you in your land, do not molest him. You must count him as one of your own countrymen and love him as yourself — for you were once strangers yourselves in Egypt." It's a straightforward command from God, predicated, of course, on correct determination of just who is the "stranger."

It's not merely a case of labeling the Arabs as the strangers, although Palestinians will certainly tell you the Jews are the strangers. Even if Biblical right of ownership is respected, which Jewish group can justify laying principal claim to the land? Is it the Sefardi aristocrats who began coming to Palestine in the 17th Century? The ultra-Orthodox Ashkenazi Haredim, those people who arrived in the mid-19th Century? Perhaps it's the secular Zionist socialists, following in the Herzl-Weizmann tradition? The Revisionists of Jabotinsky? Holocaust survivors? Iraqi Jews? Moroccan Jews? Ethiopian Jews? American Jews?

That's just the point. Today's Israel is an amalgam of peoples from more than 70 different national origins, each group conscious of its Jewishness, each one seeking to preserve its individuality while paying the in-

evitable price of assimilation. It's a veritable Tower of Babel, but somehow it works. It's First World; it's Third World. It's the frontier; it's the establishment. It's infuriating; it's lovable. Above all it's intriguing. In Israel paradox is heaped upon paradox, seasoned with irony, stirred by emergency.

To love Israel is not to unnecessarily glamorize it, to make it seem as though every rural panorama has the impact of the Grand Canyon; or to portray every citizen as a hero of Zionist labor who plows his fields all day, tends to his family all night, and reads the Bible and Bialik in between rooting for Tel Aviv Maccabee and taking his grandfather to *shul*. To use American vernacular, it just ain't so. No. To love Israel is to show it as it is and let its special, very special qualities shine through the entertaining debates of everyday life.

M ost Israelis are outspoken in their biting comments about their country's politics and politicians; like big city taxi drivers, they all know better how to govern than any of the Knesset's 120 members. Criticism of the government and society in general is a national pastime like nowhere else in the Middle East, but that's an unfair regional comparison because democracies are in short supply in that area of the planet. Paradoxically, what keeps the front pages interesting is the emotional catharsis which provides the dialogue to keep the country healthy.

There are several inescapable references which any credible book on Israel must include, and *Israel: Images & Ideas* is no exception. Dedication to building a new society, success against almost all odds, agricultural and technological pre-eminence, academic excellence, are all ineradicable elements. There is also the issue of the Palestinians, more specifically, the *Arab* Palestinians, a problem that refuses to go away.

Almost every Israeli success must be measured in terms of the Arab threats which have spawned the Israeli struggle to survive since the earliest days of the Yishuv. In the *Foreword* of this volume, Ezer Weizman has succinctly remarked that the Arabs "molded us." 40 years after independence, the Palestinian problem is still shaping the lives of every Israeli in moral, political and financial ways that can only happen in a nation which has spent its entire modern history in a state of war with its neighbors.

A quick perusal of the archival photos in this *Introduction* shows a disproportionate number of Israeli milestones to have involved men in battle. While the Arab problem has certainly accelerated development in the military/technological fields, one can only wonder how much growth it has stunted in other areas. Nothing else has so shaped the face of the country since the earliest days of the Yishuv. Nothing.

The history of modern Israel is steeped in irony and paradox. Imagine a colony with no colonial power behind it. Or sod-busting settlers with graduate degrees. How did it happen?

The failure of 19th Century European Jews to satisfactorily achieve assimilation in a Gentile society spawned the Zionist movement. Well before the Balfour Declaration of 1917 Jews were finding their way to Palestine, hoping to fulfill Theodor Herzl's dream to build a country where social responsibility would create "a light unto the nations." The development of Israel is the story of Zionism, and how those intrepid Europeans in the early *aliyot* built a country from nothing. Probably no other country was colonized with so many disadvantages, and yet so many advantages.

Ottoman Palestine offered nothing but problems to immigrants who had to produce their own food from day one. The dry, barren topography provided absolutely no resources while delivering only local hostility on the part of local Arabs and Turks. With little money and no great power's colonial office to call upon in times of trouble, early Zionists could only rely on their determination and their intellect.

These attributes were precisely their unique advantage. Unlike so many other overseas colonies which drew their initial populations from less than ideal elements of society, the Yishuv enjoyed an extremely high standard of educated immigrant. If professors and doctors had to roll up their sleeves, transforming themselves into agrarians for the first time in 2000 years of Jewish history, nevertheless intellectually they remained professors and doctors.

Accordingly Eretz Yisrael boasted a rate of applied science development unparalleled in any new territory. No sooner had the early pioneers harvested their first subsistence crops than they began to build institutes of higher education to perpetuate the advantage they brought with them. The country's first institution was an agricultural high school to train farmers, and within little more than two generations the Yishuv had become the learning center of the Middle East. Hebrew University, the Technion, and the Weizmann Institute began to attract outstanding professors from abroad, especially after the rise of Nazism in Germany. So ten years before the creation of Israel, this colony that was not a colony, this country that was not yet a country enjoyed a First World level of academic excellence.

The years between the World Wars were heady times for the Yishuv. The pioneering spirit prevailed throughout the community, as immigrants flocked in successive *aliyot* to build a land with their own hands. They took arduous manual labor as a sort of personal salvation; not only were they building a new land, they were working on a new Jewish society, a utopia where the shame of the ghetto would be expunged by the return to the soil. Early leaders conceived of an egalitarian society based on 19th Century utopian philosophies. Proudly they illustrated the apparent success of their programs by pointing to the growth of the kibbutzim, where close comradeship and socialist ideals prevailed.

But while turn-of-the-century Palestine had been a poor backwater of the Ottoman empire, it was not a vacuum. From the very beginnings of the Yishuv there was violent conflict between Zionist settlers and local Arabs. American-born West Bank settler Bob Steinberger proclaims that "the problem with the Jew is that intellectually he's very much aware of anti-Semitism over the years, and he doesn't want to be accused of the same thing. But emotionally, he says, 'I don't want to be dead...right.' And that's the problem."

In contemporary vernacular, this pinpoints one of the fundamental paradoxes of Israeli life: how to remain truly democratic and secure at the same time certain regional revolutionaries aggrandize their own images by fomenting trouble with and within Israel.

Throughout the '20s and '30s Arab leaders continued their anti-Jewish posturing, as the British Mandatory Government alternately wooed the Arabs and placated the Jews. For all their knowledge of the past, the British completely mis-read Arab history and thought they could accomplish in a decade what no Khalifa had done in a thousand years — unify the Arab people. If this meant forsaking the spirit of the Balfour Declaration and paying mere lip service to the Yishuv, then it was deemed an acceptable price for an imagined regional security around the Suez Canal and the first rights to drill for Arab petroleum.

The British never attempted to diplomatically isolate Jewish Palestine from the rest of the Arab world, although such a move would surely have allowed them to approach each problem separately. While the Foreign Office tried to placate them, Kings Feisal and Abdullah railed against further Zionist immigration, even though many of the Arab commonfolk had different ideas about their neighbors.

The Jewish community was indubitably prospering, and the allure of steady employment drew Arabs by the thousands into Palestine. Indeed Abdullah held secret talks with the Yishuv leaders in the '30s, as he attempted to attract a few Jews to Amman in efforts to stimulate the economy. In return, he permitted many Transjordanians to find work in Palestine. What must be one of modern history's greatest ironies is that many of today's rioters throw stones at the grandsons of the very people who attracted their forebears to Palestine in the first place.

Today it is difficult for an outsider to properly comprehend the Israelis' attachment to the land. Beyond the Biblical claims and secure geographical borders, is the universal love of the soil the people themselves have turned into their own breadbasket. Israeli agri-culture has become a world leader in the development of new irrigation methods, and a major exporter of fruit and flowers to the European market. Meanwhile hundreds of millions of trees have been lovingly planted to afforestate a land that had been arboreally denuded since before the Middle Ages. Only if you have planted a tree in Israel can you fully appreciate the ignominy of the wave of summer arson in 1988.

I told this one Palestinian guy that the troubles have to be over with," says American-born West Bank settler Bob Steinberger, recalling an anecdote significant for its no-win outlook on the situation. "He agrees. I say, 'Look you've got three choices. First choice: you kill all the Jews.'

"He says 'How am I gonna do that?'

"I tell him, 'Look, I'm tellin' you *what* to do, not how to do it.'

"He says, 'What's the second choice?'

"I tell him he's gotta throw all these PLO bums out.

"He says 'How am I gonna do that? They've got guns. They come in the night with Molotov cocktails and burn your house down...What's the third choice?'

"You kill yourself."

A non-cynical but no less disturbing outlook is espoused by Professor Moshe Lissak of Hebrew University. "We ask ourselves if the utopia we wanted to build here was really feasible or not. The question of the Occupied Territory and controlling the Palestinians is corrupting Israeli society. I don't know how long we can cope with it; I don't mean from a political or military point of view, but socially. That's our main problem now; we're at a watershed of Israeli history."

Whatever his political stripe, no one in Israel would dispute Professor Lissak's observation, especially in a country where almost a third of the GNP is spent on defense, notwithstanding $1.8 billion in annual American military aid. A nation that calls up all its reservists for 35-60 days a year *every year* has some hard questions to answer. It remains to be seen just how much of their past Israelis are willing to relinquish in order to put right their future. ∎

BELOW: Laying water pipe in the Negev, Kibbutz Sde Boker, 1954.
BOTTOM: Draining swamps by Lake Hula, 1953.

*Field workers returning home after work, Emer Hefer, 1935.*

*ABOVE: Steel helmeted riot police going into action outside Government House in Jaffa against Arab rioters protesting large Jewish immigration from Germany, October 1933.*
*OPPOSITE: Sergeant Pressman disarming an Arab marauder; Hashomer watchman with an ancient shotgun, ca. 1910; ploughing continues even though boiler plate must be added to the tractors because of snipers.*

Technion students strength-
testing materials, 1936; aerial
view of the first moshav, Nahalal,
founded in 1921 and arranged
like the spokes of a wheel.
OPPOSITE: Camels loaded with
gravel boxes, working on the Tel
Aviv seashore construction
project, 1936.

A unit of "Samson's Foxes" in 1948 during the War of Independence. Note the collection of leftover World War II equipment: American Jeep and tommy gun, German machine gun, British rifle and helmets. BELOW: Unable to purchase any artillery, the Haganah resorted to home-made mortars like this crude but effective welding shop product.

*A convoy of home-made armored vehicles running the Arab gantlet on the way to re-supply Jerusalem in 1948. LEFT: Israeli forward positions in Jerusalem's Yemin Moshe district in 1948; just west of what would be the Green Line.*

*Israel's flag flutters over the crowded upper decks of the Haganah ship "Exodus" in Haifa Harbor before the immigrants were turned away by the British. July 1947. OPPOSITE: Immigrants from Aden on plane, 1943; Moshe Raymond from India learns to read Hebrew in the IDF; survivors of European detention camps after arrival in Atlit reception center, November 1944.*

El Al's first Constellation,
December 1950.

The plant interior of the Assia
Pharmaceuticals plant,
November 1949 (now part of Teva
Pharmaceutical Industries).
OPPOSITE: laying the
National Water Carrier in the
Sharon Valley, June 1959.

OPPOSITE: General Motta Gur's paratroops at the Western Wall after the recapture of Jerusalem, June 1967.
ABOVE: An Egyptian armored column destroyed by Israeli aircraft at Mitla Pass in the Sinai desert, June 5, 1967; Generals Moshe Dayan and Yitzhak Rabin entering Jerusalem through St. Stephen's Gate, June 7, 1967.

OPPOSITE: Burning Egyptian refineries at Suez after Israeli
shelling during the War of Attrition, October 1968; American-
made M-60 tanks advance in Sinai during the Yom Kippur
War, October 1973.
ABOVE: Anwar Sadat and Menachem Begin greeting each
other at dinner at Jerusalem's King David Hotel during
Sadat's historic peace-seeking visit to Israel, November 1977.

*Daybreak in the Old City.*

# ARISE, SHINE OUT

*Aerial photo of Jerusalem taken in 1937 under the British Mandate. Hebrew University and Hadassah Hospital on Mt. Scopus (top right) represent the only significant construction north of the Old City. There has been no afforestation as yet. The area by the Western Wall is a clutter of small houses, and immediately to the west is the old Jewish Quarter before it was despoiled by the Jordanians during their 19 years of occupation, 1948-67. Of note (lower left, near the Cardo) is the venerable Hurva Synagogue, with its distinctive arch.*

*Contemporary Jerusalem. Mt. Scopus now seems covered
with the Hebrew University complex, and the dramatic effects
of the afforestation program are evident. The Western Wall is
cleared, the Jewish Quarter and the Cardo have been
reconstructed. Sadly several old structures remain only as
shells, notably the Hurva Synagogue.*

ARISE, SHINE OUT, FOR YOUR LIGHT has come; the glory of Yaweh is rising on you, though night still covers the earth and darkness the peoples," the Prophet Isaiah has invoked his beloved Jerusalem for 25 centuries. At the crossroads of three continents, this mother of cities is sacred to the three great monotheistic Western religions as the site of the Temple, the Crucifixion, and Muhammad's ascent to Heaven.

From its inception as a Hebrew hill town some 3,000 years ago, Jerusalem has evoked both unparalleled religious fervor and belligerent emotions. "It's a focus of unity, but a crossroads of conflict," remarks bookseller Noah Kaplan. "It's been the the blood-soaked victim of conquests by countless armies and empires....Assyrians, Babylonians, Persians, Greeks, Romans, Khaliffas and Crusaders, Ottomans and English have sacked and pillaged, slaughtered and enslaved, built and beautified here," details Kaplan. "All in the name of God."

Since 1967 Jerusalem has been united under Israeli rule; today it is effectively three cities under one municipal jurisdiction. To the west is largely modern, Jewish Jerusalem, Israel's capital since 1980 and studded with high rises, modern developments and green parks. To the east is Arab Jerusalem, where the dusty, crowded villages — many still lacking modern sewage systems — stand in stark contrast to such gargantuan modern complexes like Hebrew University on Mt. Scopus. In the middle is the Old City, "the essence of Jerusalem," as Kaplan puts it. "Visitors can find at least a common attraction to the Holy Places even if their religions cannot yet find common political ground," he notes with a sigh.

It's enormously picturesque, but there's an irony even about Old Jerusalem's photogeneity. "Tell me why is it that photographers always make pictures of churches and mosques; almost never of synagogues?" queries IDF Captain Eliyahu Revat, who spends his off-duty times home in Netanya. "It is strange to find a Jewish state where the tourist photographs the temples of the other religions.

"What is Judaism — perhaps 2000 years older than Christianity, 2600 years older than Islam — so why is it so distinctly non-photogenic?" muses Revat.

"When I am in Jerusalem I see tourists with cameras; most of them I think are Jews, but most of them photograph the Dome of the Rock, the Church of the Holy Sepulchre. It is very strange to me, Jews coming to the Holy City of their religious heritage but mostly photographing the places of the Gentiles."

The holiest place in Judaism is the Western Wall, all that remains of the retaining wall around Herod's Second Temple. "The accidents of history have left the Jews very little today," says television cameraman David Ben Meir with a wry smile. "There are many worshipped places, but the buildings on those spots are only memorials of an earlier period. Look at it, the famous Western Wall," he continues with a shrug. "Fifty meters of stone blocks; not very impressive, not very beautiful. But it's *original*, how do you say it — 'the real thing?' And now it belongs to us."

What is and what is not the "real thing" provides a source for ongoing debate, especially with Christian Holy Places, where the authenticity of many has been called to question. "People see what they wish to see," observes Jerusalem art dealer Simcha Meyer, tilting his head and mustering a faint smile. "When they visit the Coenaculum, or Room of the Last Supper, people overlook the documented fact that what they see is a 14th Century Franciscan restoration. Since the time of St. Helena the Christian sects have been unable to resist smothering their Biblical sites with chapels and monuments of their own to the point where the site itself has ceased to identifiably exist. Teddy Kollek says it is not, but this city is really a museum where every group is its own curator," concludes Meyer. Curiously, the only indisputably original items remaining from the time of Jesus are *still alive*: eight venerable olive trees in the Garden of Gethsemane.

Here in the narrow streets, bazaars and markets thrive in the very shadows of the Holy Places which draw so many of their customers. Here one can step back 100 years into an authentic *sukh* of the Middle East, or stroll the thoroughly modern Jewish Quarter, completely rebuilt after the '67 War. "Like any tourist attraction, the Old City has its tacky aspects," comments visitor Zevulon Cohen from Tel Aviv. "Look at the 'Third Station T-shirt Shop.' Show me any active monument and I'll show you commercialism. Yes, the Via Dolorosa is now sorrowful for additional reasons, but you cannot blame the local peoples for creating their own employment," he concedes.

Self-appointed guides, panhandlers and souvenir shops abound; young Arab boys hustle beads they swear are really mother of pearl. "See the Bedouin grazing their sheep and goats in the parks around the Old City walls?" Cohen asks rhetorically. "It's all part of the unbelievable mosaic of Jerusalem. It is a small United Nations where every diversity will be found within the radius of a few city blocks."

Here children of more than 70 different national origins play their improvised games on the cobbled streets while their parents can only wonder at the sort of world they will grow up into. "It's a problematic city in a problematic country," comments Orthodox Rabbi and City Council Member Meir Porush. "Minorities always have that feeling of discrimination, that's why there are so many upsurges of emotions."

"Above all Jerusalem has never lost its ability to evoke heated passions," reflects Simcha Meyer on the city of his birth. "Before the '67 reunification, this was a sad, rundown city, divided by the infamous Green Line which left the Old City and East Jerusalem split from the western city by barbed wire and minefields."

"Beginning in 1948 Jordanian snipers, up in the parapets of the Old City walls, shot at people across the Green Line in charming old quarters like Yemin Moshe," recalls Mayor Teddy Kollek's press liasion Sevanah Meryn sadly. "So Yemin Moshe became a deserted slum. Free access to the Holy Places, all under Jordanian control, was irregular for Christians, prohibited to Jews. In many ways it was like Berlin, only worse because there was state of war between Israel and Jordan. And unfortunately there still is."

**Y**et despite the ongoing political struggles swirling over and around its municipal boundaries, today's reunited Jerusalem exudes a new hope in the person of its mayor of 21 years, Teddy Kollek. Although he administers a population of 500,000 widely diverse peoples, Kollek firmly believes his people can live in harmony without necessarily loving each other or seeking assimilation.

"The error that many make is to want integration," he has said on many occasions. "Do you think the Armenians want to integrate? They came here to remain Armenians in the city of Christ. They have remained Armenians under all previous rulers, and now under the Israelis," he notes.

"Kollek is the supreme realist!" exclaims Progressive Rabbi Asher Hurwitz, long-time Jerusalem resident now living in Tel Aviv. "Teddy coaxes and cajoles his peoples into making the city work even though they have no other basis for coexisting within themselves."

Although his Jerusalem Foundation has raised over $180 million from mostly Jewish benefactors in the Diaspora, Kollek insists that non-Jewish areas receive their fair share of Foundation munificence. Thus he pushes ahead with plans for additional hospitals, schools, libraries and cultural activities in Arab East Jerusalem despite the fact that he has received not a penny from wealthy Arabs.

"This is a land where political and religious polarizations come all too easily," explains Rabbi Hurwitz, "but Kollek has successfully negotiated the labyrinths of special interest groups as no other politician has ever done. He's a secular Jew, you know," says Hurwitz, "made aliyah in the '30s, I think. And he insists that his city has room for all who want to live in peace."

Kollek is 76 years old, yet his peripatetic schedule would put to shame most public figures many years his junior. And he is utterly fearless. In a land where threats and assassinations are commonplace, where political figures are, of necessity, surrounded by swarms of armed security men, Kollek ventures alone into even the poorest Arab villages. The Municipality includes 127,000 Palestinians, and he never forgets they are his citizens as well.

"Teddy Kollek is the one man who should be Prime Minister of all Israel. And all the West Bank as well," proclaims camel driver Khalil Naihmi of the Mt. of Olives Village. "The Shamir people and the Gush Emunim people and the Mea She'arim people hate Teddy Kollek because he refuses to stand for one people over another, for Jews over Arabs. He is for true democracy," Naihmi continues, unafraid to have his views overheard by other Palestinians who might brand him a collaborator.

"I tell you that he has come here to our village at least two thousand times. He comes in his small car with no bodyguards, no machine guns. He walks the streets without any fear at all, and he talks to everybody. He eats his dinner in our houses and he asks us what we will need for our schools and hospitals and clubs for the old aged people. Any person who says he does not like Teddy Kollek is a person who does not like democracy. That is a person who *needs* to have a machine gun because he has so many enemies!"

"Essentially Teddy is a self-proclaimed pragmatist, willing to trade concessions by one group for compromises by another," comments bank teller Yehezkel Sarid. "He is a realistic influence broker who tries to make all parties see the light of knowing and respecting their limits.

"You must realize that politics is a dirty practice," adds Sarid with a shrug. "So for all his egalitarian views Kollek has often been the target of extremists on both sides. Today, the nationalistic Jewish Right condemns him for being open-handed to the Arabs. Tomorrow, Palestinian hard-liners who wish to radicalize their people say Kollek is provocative so they can make them more supportive of the *intifada*.

"Look, Teddy does not back away from anybody," says Sarid, proudly supporting his mayor. "He went against the Vatican when the Romans wanted internationalization of the city. He will not shut down our city streets on Sabbath. He was with Hillel Bardin's demonstration to protest more government seizure of land and the uprooting of Arab olive trees in Sur Bahir Village. And once Teddy did a sitdown strike on the steps of the Knesset to get his soccer stadium!"

Avraham Shor made aliyah 11 years ago from his native Montreal; today he owns an ice cream bar not far from city hall and talks about his mayor. "His coalition ticket is virtually unchallenged. His enormous political stature has made him virtually untouchable at the polls. Only a crazy man would run against him. So what do *I* think of Teddy? Listen, anybody who wishes to be mayor of this city has to be a masochist. Everybody's always on his back. They phone at all hours with all sorts of complaints because his residence number is in the book.

"But there is this one fellow, Michael Kramer. He is from Chicago and he is campaigning for the mayor's office and the City Council. 100,000 shekels they say he is spending, and he does not even speak Hebrew! In the Jewish Quarter of the Old City he is the committee member for garbage collection, so now he thinks he can direct the whole Municipality. He says you must be of low intelligence to be in politics, and perhaps he is correct when he talks of himself. Look at these advertisements he puts in the newspaper: IT IS NOT KRAMER VERSUS KRAMER, IT IS KRAMER FOR JERUSALEM. IT IS NOT TALK, IT IS RESULTS THAT COUNT. "I believe he has good intentions, but I think maybe he expects the voters to be as stupid as he is."

Kollek's Advisor on East Jerusalem Affairs, Amir Cheshin, puts it more simply. "Teddy Kollek is the greatest mayor in the world. I say that not because he's my boss, but because he's doing a great job. It would be a waste for him to become Prime Minister or stand for the Knesset instead of doing a great job in Jerusalem." Curiously the mayor is still saddled with legislative burdens that make his challenging task all the more difficult. "Here we have to struggle along under legislation derived from the British Mandatory Municipal Code of 1934," laments Cheshin. "Authority on the city budget remains with the national government, which does not as yet provide additional funding to compensate the Municipality for its capital status."

And while he indisputably commands the respect of almost everybody, Kollek does not even command his own local police force. "In Israel we have a national police force," explains Cheshin. "The headquarters are here in Jerusalem, but the force is not under the control of the mayor, nor is the chief of the Jerusalem police appointed by the mayor," he says, somewhat ruefully, before quickly adding. "But especially in view of the current problems, the relationship between the police force and the Municipality is very good. We have meetings all the time when there are problems."

These are the unfortunate times of the *intifada*, the general term for the Palestinian uprising which began in the West Bank and Gaza in December 1987. Emotions run high these days, as Jamal Dawar, a vegetable seller in East Jerusalem voices. "Why do you Americans come here? These are bad times for us, and your country only makes it worse by supporting the Jews. We do not hate you, but if your tourist dollars were not paid to the Israelis then they would feel the *real* pressure of the intifada. Then they would be forced to give us back our land.

"You think the Syrians and the Jordanians are telling us what to do, but you are wrong. The Palestinian people have a righteous cause, and even your government senators admit it, while in the same breath they tell us to get new leaders with which they may talk."

Fortunately for Jerusalem, Dawar and his people are able to differentiate between Kollek's leadership and the policies of the national government. "I tell you that I do not like being told by the intifada to shut up my store here, but I recognize it is required to put pressure on the Israelis. Even more I do not like the police telling us to close during hours when our leaders tell us to open. These police are not Teddy Kollek's police; they are Shamir's police. They think they can last longer than us in this opening and closing battle. But they are mistaken. The Palestinian people have suffered much greater humiliations and difficulties, and

they will be the ones to finally decide."

Other Palestinians concede that the 21 years of Israeli rule in Jerusalem have provided significant job opportunities never available before. And while many are sympathetic to the cause of the intifada, they manage to work around it, as does this Sherut driver from Issawaya Village: "Most certainly things are good for my taxi business. Without the Jews there would be little work here. Is there any tourism in Jordan? Any big business in Amman? No.

"I am the owner of this taxi now; things go well for me. Every night I return home to Issawaya going by way of Silwan, so if any of my friends see my car along the road they will not think I have been carrying Israeli passengers or violating the general strikes called by the leaders of the intifada."

The unavoidable spillover of West Bank strikes and riots has been comparatively minor in the Arab neighborhoods of East Jerusalem, a testament to Kollek's popularity. While they risk reproach from their fellow Arabs for "legitimizing" Israeli government by participating in elections, more than 30% of the men do so they can re-elect Teddy. Nevertheless Kollek's greatest problem remains that of his Arab constituents, and often this requires his personal intervention.

"Recently the police intervened after disturbances following the Friday prayers on the Temple Mount. They burned an American flag; they burned an Israeli flag and rioting began," relates Amir Cheshin. "The police used tear gas and rubber bullets, and immediately Teddy's office began to get complaints from the Muslim authorities.

"The situation was extremely explosive. Nevertheless Teddy decided he'd like to go see the Mufti, the head of the Islamic hierarchy on the Temple Mount. This man plays two roles; he's the head of the Islamic authority, as well as the Mufti, or head of religious functions. So Teddy had a visit to the Mufti, who showed him the tear gas grenades. According to his version, they were thrown into the morning prayers at Al-Aksa Mosque," Cheshin relates. "It was not true, by the way, but nevertheless Teddy had a dialogue with the Mufti.

And since that day we had more than two months of absolute quiet around the Temple Mount."

While Western newsmen oversimplify what they think is a monolithic structure of Palestinian leadership, nothing could be farther from the truth. Curiously, it is Palestinian disunity that may be the greatest cause of unrest. "Our biggest problem is the lack of coordination between the Arabs themselves," Cheshin confirms. "As well as the fear from known or unknown organizations who undermine the coexistence which we are trying to build in the city."

Resolutely Cheshin insists on the unified nature of Jerusalem. "People say that the city is still divided. I've been in only two divided cities in my life, Beirut and Berlin. There I saw the real meaning of a divided city. Jerusalem is not divided. We definitely know that there is a general Arab willingness to live together with Jews. Jews and Arabs have lived together in this area of the Middle East for centuries, and lived in Jerusalem with whatever we call coexistence," he adds.

**D**avid Arkush is a local banker who sees money as one of the key issues in Arab-Jewish relations. "A big obstacle to future relations is the fiscal policy of the central government. They never dispense sufficient money for the essential services Kollek's people would like to provide the Arabs in East Jerusalem," Arkush explains. "There, without the comparative affluence of West Jerusalem, without outside benefactors, the problems are staggering."

Amir Cheshin agrees. "There is so much more to do in the construction of schools for the Arab children; in providing sewer systems to several neighborhoods which don't have them yet; in finishing the infrastructure in the Old City — which is not finished yet; and many other issues for which we desperately need money," he laments. "And this money has to come out of the national budget."

Even when vitally needed items are given outright to the city, usually from the Diaspora, "the national government's strangling and inconsistent tax structure intervenes," complains Warren Brodsky, therapist for handicapped children. "Listen, American Jews think they're giving money to Israel for this or that, but I can tell you that most of that money never gets through to the children it's supposed to help. American Jews give to United Jewish Appeal, for instance, but here it just goes into the Israel Allied Fund where it's given to some great bureaucracy and disappears.

"And even when they give, say an ambulance, they don't know that there's a 135% tax on it when it gets here. The government makes no exceptions, not even for humanitarian gifts. I know some cases where equipment had to be returned because there wasn't the money to pay the import duties. That's how you get a $20,000 ambulance which ends up costing $47,000. It's crazy, but the government just wants its ridiculous profits even if it means giving up important equipment for needy causes."

"I think it's the capricious unpredictability of the Israeli tax collectors which causes a great deal of trouble," opines graphic artist David Greene, an English immigrant. "One year I might pay about NIS 10,000 in taxes, the next they ask me for 35,000 although I won't have made any more money!"

National government parsimony and tax irregularities notwithstanding, Teddy manages to keep up a schedule of local improvement and beautification that would embarrass mayors with ten times his budget. With precious little funding from the national government, he relies on his Jerusalem Foundation and almost universal goodwill to make his city function, to make ends come closer to meeting.

"Yes, the Jerusalem Foundation helps a great deal," elaborates Amir Cheshin, "but there are restrictions to the money. The Foundation, for example, will never allocate money for paving roads. It will never give us money for a new sewer system."

"Our systems are antiques, and overloaded antiques at that. Basically the country is too poor to fix its telephone system, its road system, even the sewer systems in some of the outlying villages," complains Jerusalem accountant Miriam Mendes. "If one of your American health inspectors went to many of the local

Arab villages, he would have them closed down as dangers to public health. Yes, it's that serious."

Certainly Mendes' views are in keeping with prevailing attitudes in city hall. "From time to time the Arabs raise the point that their sections of the city do not receive sufficient funding," concedes Amir Cheshin. "At the same time their official position is that they do not recognize the reunification of 1967. But they also approach it from the other direction when they want something. Then they tell me, 'Listen, this is a reunified city now. No matter what the intifada does, you can't have part of the city open and part of it closed. You have to do something about it.' And then later in the media they blame me personally for persuading the military authorities or the police to force the merchants to open their stores."

Today Arabs constitute a high percentage of Jerusalem's semi-skilled labor force; over 30,000 commute into the city just to fill the jobs nobody else will do. As a group, Arabs represent the low end of the income scale, and for them Israel's budget troubles compound the East Jerusalem problems. "The Arabs think that for the taxes they pay they should get all their services free. Unfortunately the system in Israel is slightly different," explains Cheshin. "We've had many places in the western part of the city where residents wanted to pave a road or a sidewalk, and they have paid extra fees to the city to get these jobs done. Sometimes we face problems in collecting money for extra services, but we forgive the debt, and the national government realize that some of the money which goes to East Jerusalem will never be received back in the form of taxes — as is the custom elsewhere."

The immediate outlook for this east-west inequality is not particularly bright, and many Arab areas of the city are likely to stay run-down until those local residents can upgrade their own financial status. "Jerusalem is by far the poorest municipality among the three big cities," Cheshin explains. "We don't have a special budget for being the capital. We collect taxes and this is our budget. We get allowances from the ministry, as every other municipality, according to the number of residents." And unless a generous donor sees fit to fund an East Jerusalem project, many community needs go unfilled. "The Jerusalem Foundation has no money," observes Cheshin, trying to explain why an organization that raised $18 million alone in 1987 cannot always provide even a local clinic. "The Foundation receives donations earmarked for specific projects. I might even say that most donors do not give money for projects in the Arab section. Nevertheless I don't know how the city could manage without the money the Foundation *does* allocate for institutions and important activities in East Jerusalem."

To test the waters of Palestinian philanthropy, Amir Cheshin had an idea several years ago: why not create an East Jerusalem Foundation, specifically aimed at Arab culture and needs. "I met with rich Arabs with good contacts, and I proposed to them to send one of their number to the Palestinian diaspora in America," he relates. "I've had the chance to meet many very wealthy Palestinians who have come through here from America or Europe. And they are stuffed with money; some own chains of supermarkets.

"Now one man I met was a very rich person. He was very excited and thought the idea was wonderful. He asked what this new foundation might do, for what purpose its money would be spent. I said we desperately needed a school in Sawachra, a poor southern Jerusalem neighborhood. He told me I was crazy. 'You expect me to collect money in America for these Bedouins who are living without work in Jerusalem?'

"'Originally they were Bedouins, perhaps a hundred years ago, but they settled,' I told him. 'These people are Arabs, and they're proud Palestinians. Maybe more Palestinian than you! While your children have a wonderful school in America, these children have no school at all.'

"So he said, 'Listen, nobody would give a penny for this purpose. If you want to build a country club or a swimming pool or a playground in Sheikh Jarrah, near the American Colony, for this we might raise money.'

"So even for schools we cannot raise money. In the

near future we want to build a public library center in East Jerusalem with money raised by Teddy Kollek through the Jerusalem Foundation. So Teddy offered to a group of notables from East Jerusalem the chance to run the center even before it started — to be involved in the construction, the planning, the activities. I'm still waiting for people to approach me, but so far there has been no response."

Tell stories like this to Palestinians, and their responses are predictably short, similar to politically-oriented disclaimers elsewhere in the Arab world. "Why should our people help the goddam Jews build schools which they will take over for themselves?" responded an East Jerusalem doctor. "Besides, even if we bought only food for our poorer brothers and sisters we would be labeled as collaborators!" In this land of no-peace-no war, collaboration still has to be a one-way street for most Palestinians.

**J**erusalem is a city living on charity, on begging letters, on collections," Chaim Weizmann wrote nearly 80 years ago, and the pattern of economic survival continues today. If the East Jerusalem Foundation is still a gleam in Kollek's eye, the original Jerusalem Foundation has been one of his greatest success stories. "The main goal of the Foundation is to make Jerusalem a better place to live; that doesn't only include buildings and parks but also social and educational things of vital importance," declares Foundation spokesman Barri Avnerre.

"We have benefactors who donate their money for specific projects," explains Avnerre. "The way we work is that we get requests mainly through the Municipality and we work out our priorities, Jerusalem's priorities.

"Although our immediate needs are sometimes more difficult to fund than aesthetic cultural projects which receive more articles in the media, the Foundation has nevertheless managed to help bridge the gap caused by national government cutbacks in public health and services for the aged," outlines Avnerre.

Above all, the Foundation is the leader of the Jerusalem renaissance. From sculptures to school rooms, playgrounds to parks, puppet theaters to public institutions, the Foundation has completed over 900 projects — including such diverse works as the renovation of no less than 170 synagogues, 10 mosques, an international puppet festival, an organ for the Dormition Abbey and a central TV antenna for the Muslim Quarter in the Old City.

"We plan each project, determine its costs, and then interest benefactors in the undertaking," he continues, noting that the Foundation tries to interest donors in projects that are very close to their personal interests.

Obviously the system works, unabashedly playing on the overt desire to have one's own slice of Jerusalem marked with one's personal plaque. "Donors are more likely to give money when they can get their name on it," Avnerre explains.

"Over the past 22 years we have received over $180 million; over the last year alone we raised $18 million. Donors are mainly from abroad, 40% from the United States, but we also have Foundation Boards in England, Canada and West Germany."

Like Cheshin, Avnerre laments the unequal status of East Jerusalem projects. "One of our main problems is that we didn't do enough there, but what we have done is still working, even in these days of trouble. We have a lot of sports fields, youth clubs and community centers, all working and active," he notes. "Projects in East Jerusalem are going ahead, however, and we do have joint Jewish-Arab projects. We have also a center for the blind and a lot of work going on at the Museum of Natural History. We don't get any criticism from the Government for what we do.

"Despite the intifada, none of our projects in East Jerusalem has been defaced or vandalized. If someone would give the Foundation $10 million for East Jerusalem, I would first of all build more classrooms for the Arab schools, secondly computerize the schools, then build community centers. I think these would be the priorities of the Foundation; if we had the grants. Had we been able to do more, I think the troubles might have been less," Avnerre opines as he wonders why the Foundation has not one Arab donor.

"They seem to be afraid of being identified with something Israeli, even though this is the Jerusalem Foundation not the Israeli Foundation. We do nothing outside of Jerusalem. We have Christian and Jewish donors but no Muslims, no Arabs," he adds sadly.

"These days we try to maintain a low profile right now in East Jerusalem, we recently had an opening of a health center. Deliberately it wasn't publicized so that the fellow who works there wouldn't have his picture on TV. Then he might have problems because he lives and works with Israelis," adds Avnerre with more than a touch of frustration.

Breaking into a wide smile, Avnerre outlines the Foundation's most ambitious project to-date. "We have a huge project now which we call Bible Valley, linking the Valleys of Kidron and Hinnom. It will be a park extending halfway way around the Old City with many pathways linking existing archaeological sites with others yet to be restored. This Municipality has a more concentrated collection of archaeological history than anywhere else in the world."

**B**ut even digging for a public works project faces unusual problems in Jerusalem, where ultra-Orthodox Haredim and certain Muslim groups are always ready to protest.

"I believe it was 1981 when the troubles began," relates archaelogical student David Wasserstein. "Some Haredim jumped into the City of David digs; they climbed into the holes to protest desecration of possible Jewish graves 3000 years old. Of course, nobody had found any bones, but the slightest possibility started them up...There are so few of them, but they have so much influence in the Knesset," he exclaimed. "So they got through a bill to stop all digging if human bones were found. And if the Chief Rabbinate then said the bones were Jewish, then the dig would have to be closed up!"

"Here the Orthodox have a complete monopoly on everything," gripes Leo Bernstein, a former kibbutznik who has now returned to his native New York. "Without them you can't get married, divorced, or converted.

Our Reform rabbis can't even serve in the IDF as chaplains! If the fate of Israel had been left to a bunch of yeshiva students, the Arabs would have swallowed up this country the next day," Bernstein opines.

"When I look at the amount of money that comes from the States to support Israel, from Reform congregations in America, it makes me sick to see how little respect the Reform Movement —they call it "Progressive" over here — gets.

"Look at Jerusalem. This whole town shuts down on Friday evenings. Do you think New York closes down then? Of course not. All the Jews are out having dinner — and probably not a Kosher one at that. Yet they're still good Jews, proud of our history and traditions," Bernstein observes. "Do you know when the first Reform congregation was formed in Jerusalem? 1958! Not until then. We got off worse than the goyim!"

**D**espite their objections on other matters, the Orthodox community, especially the Haredi, concede that the city gives them all they want. "Every minority feels the majority wants to discriminate against it. It's a psychological fact that a minority always has a chip on its shoulder. So a minority will always look to form a coalition with those who will fulfill its needs," explains Rabbi Meir Porush.

"The Haredi minority is different. It's not like the majority of citizens' rights movements, or like the other minorities in the city," Porush acknowledges with matter-of-fact pride. "We get all the facilities we need, children's clinics, community clinics, etc. Ours is a different type of minority."

Although there is no recent census, current estimates put the number of Jerusalem Haredim at 57,000, slightly over 11% of the total population but nevertheless disproportionately rewarded with 10 out of 31 seats on the City Council. "But almost 7000 Haredim do not participate at all in government," notes school teacher Shulamit Lubimov. "You know, they don't even recognize the State of Israel yet," she exclaims disdainfully.

"They call themselves the *Neturei Karta*. They

hate Zionists, pay no taxes, don't serve in the army and boycott all elections. They think that only God can authorize a state for the Jewish people. Before the intifada, you know," she continued, "they tried to stop traffic on Shabbat by stoning passing cars. Imagine!"

"Ideologically they do not vote," comments Rabbi Porush. "They believe they can't operate under a Government that is not completely structured under the Torah. They don't vote because they believe it was wrong to establish the State, because it would cause problems with the Arabs, problems with the world community and so on."

But common threats have a way of changing at least *some* behavior patterns. "As soon as the uprising started, even those crazy people said that's it," comments an IDF major at a news stand on Jaffa Road. "The police shouldn't have to put their resources into the fight between secular and religious Jews.

"You know," he continued, "it's like any other country. When things outside are quiet, then we'll fight a civil war. But when things become too violent, then we'll unite. I suspect that everybody knows where his limits are, what his ultimate problems of survival are."

"Tell that to the PLO!" interjects the news vendor after a long silence. "Look at this here! Look! The *Neturei Karta* bastards want to close the pornographic shop in the Beit Clal, so they are writing to Arafat! To Arafat!" he explodes, shaking his copy of *Ha'aretz* in the air. "They want to have Arafat tell the UN to come clean out the city!"

Indeed the special status of the Haredi and Orthodox in general often evoke bitter resentment, especially in Jerusalem where their numbers are so visible. "The worst thing Ben-Gurion ever did was make a deal with the Orthodox, because he misunderstood his own secular Zionism," comments Jerusalem businessman Yigael Sheretz. "Back in 1949 he decided to kiss the Orthodox asses and let their 500 Yeshiva students out of army service. So these odd fellows took everything, risked nothing, and contributed not a thing to the growth of the country."

Even Teddy himself has been known to lose patience with some of the Haredim. "Yes, the story I think is true," acknowledges Sevanah Meryn, referring to the time when there was a big fire in Mea She'arim. "Teddy was in a meeting one evening, and somebody burst into the office to report the Mea She'arim fire. 'Good!' said Teddy. 'I hope the whole place burns down!'"

But if you put the question of religious vs. secular to the Haredim, their response is often more equivocal, indeed political. "Between Jews and Jews there never has been a struggle. Yes, there is a constant argument and discussion how we as Jews should live, should lead the country," says Rabbi Porush. "If we're a nation like all nations or we're the chosen nation, there are always certain responsibilities to the Torah.

"I suggest that the secular community may have a belief that they are inferior to the religious Jew, with his traditions of the past. Also they may be anxious because they see the rapidly growing birthrate of the religious community."

The birthrate issue is a hot conversation topic all over Israel, but where racial-religious differences are as great and diverse as they are in Jerusalem, secular attitudes often seem as concerned over the high Orthodox birthrate as they are over Arab population increase. "Look, *habibi*, go to Mea She'arim or Kerem Avraham. Go even to Ge'ula and you see all the young mothers with four, five, six children," notes jeweler Shaul Ben Shlomo. "Not even the Arab families have that many. That is the reason those neighborhoods are so crowded with people. And also why they are so poor and ask so much money from the National Insurance."

"Early marriages and large families are virtually institutionalized in the Orthodox community," remarks American-born Bob Sigal, fund raiser for the Bayit Lepletot Girls' Orphanage in Mea She'arim. "Within traditional Orthodox Jewish society, when a girl is pregnant what she is really praying for is a boy, a religious scholar. Most girls are delighted to have their husbands study all day long, so therefore they see nothing wrong with being the family wage-earner.

"At 18 the girls usually get married, build a house

of their own and have children. They marry boys mostly from the yeshivas. The original orphanage here was started with children that were Holocaust survivors, and the emphasis was to have more children. There was a tremendous push, from a religious perspective, to re-propagate the race.

"Here marriages are arranged through what is known as a *sheduki*. They're like marriage-brokers or matchmakers, and that's how our girls are introduced to somebody. We have a dowry fund here and often we end up making the wedding — which is a least a couple of thousand dollars. Sometimes we have to help them buy an apartment because economics and sociology here are such that unless you help these kids get started, they're never going to get married.

"As far as the Orthodox community is concerned, you have the opposite of what you have in the States where the man is considered the bread winner. A lot of the people here in Mea She'arim will earn just enough money to survive; that's all they're interested in. Some are wealthy, some are very poor," he adds.

"Excepting Shabbat, Haredim drive automobiles, ride electric elevators, use computers. But you cannot correctly consider them in Western terms. Assuredly it is wrong to evaluate their attitudes, their conduct by Western standards," ponders Jerusalem public relations executive Lev Sondek.

Sunday morning, 9:00 AM in the Old City. A small group of black-clad Armenian clergy have just begun their weekly procession to the Church of the Holy Sepulchre. "I think the police were supposed to block off the traffic," relates Italian photographer Silvio DiStefano, "but there were no police that day. Most of the approaching cars pulled over for the 30 seconds it was required for the Armenians to pass, but there was this one auto. My God! He drove directly into the procession, knocking some of the priests aside!" the Italian describes. "The driver had one of those black hats and long sidecurls; obviously he was Orthodox. Immediately a fight broke out. Some of the younger priests tried to drag the driver out of the car.

" 'You see what they do to us?' shouted one of the priests to me. 'They wish to expel us from this land!' "

"Unfortunately the city's Christian community is dwindling; there's only about 12,000 remaining," laments Benedictine Father Dominique LeBoeuf. "Traditionally Jerusalem has been a Christian intellectual center, but with less money from sources abroad, you now have a Christian exodus which began back in 1948," he notes.

"Today we Christians find ourselves in a difficult position. We're caught between Jews and Muslims, but maintaining our own identity is impossible when we have 30 different sects unwilling to cooperate with each other," Father LeBoeuf sighs. "It is the worst possible advertisement for Christianity when there is fighting between sects, especially about ridiculous things like who has a right to clean what part of the stonework in the Church of the Holy Sepulchre.

"With only 110,000 believers in the entire country, we Christians have little hope of ever achieving political power. 90% of Israeli Christians are Arabs, including the Anglican Bishop Samuel Kafriti and the Baptist Bishop Nai'im Khoury," Father LeBoeuf reflects. "Observe the Christian countries in the West. They have been always been staunch supporters of Israel. But here is the irony: Christian *individuals* in Israel have not always been pro-Israel. Their big Arab numbers make their loyalty suspect," explains LeBoeuf.

"When Christians need something done, we are learning to follow the examples set by the Jewish majority. We send home for money." And in the cases of the Greeks, the Ethiopians, the Syrians, the Armenians, the Russians, "home" — if there still is one — has little money to send.

Things weren't always so difficult for the resident Christians, especially for the Armenians, for whom Jerusalem has been a spiritual homeland since the terrible Turkish massacres of 1914-5. "The very best time for Armenians in Palestine was during the British Mandate when there were over 15,000 of us here," recalls Armenian Bishop Guregh Kapikian, himself Jerusalem-born.

"When General Allenby entered Jerusalem in 1917, there were only 1,000 Armenians here; soon 14,000 more came as refugees, escaping the massacres by the Turks. They were welcomed by the British; this was the center of our own diaspora. Jobs were plentiful for our people during the Mandate; at one time 60 Armenians worked in Barclay's Bank," he notes.

During the 1948 War, the Bishop remembers that the Armenian monastery hosted over 4,000 refugees; today only 200 live within the old walls surrounding the beautiful Crusader-era Cathedral of St. James.

"Christianity is a bit in danger," comments Bishop Guregh. "Many of the Greeks in the Old City are leaving, and without financial help from the outside, most Christians cannot afford housing. So they must leave."

With a house as bitterly divided as the Israeli Knesset, the politically powerless Christian community continues to be its own worst enemy. "There is some understanding among the Christian communities here, but each one lives its separate life. We have always lacked overall unity, and even now there are still many arguments over the Holy Places. There is no prominent Christian figure in the local government who stands out, and unfortunately we have no official connections with Jewish or Islamic authorities," notes the Bishop.

"I think the day may come when we no longer have a Christian community here in Jerusalem. Teddy Kollek is a very good friend, but now we are a tiny minority without any political influence and caught in the struggle between the Jews and the Muslims."

"Our presence here is seen as a Gentile tourist attraction by the Israelis," comments visiting Dominican Father Michael Bruno. "Here there is a cool toleration for our minorities, principally because many of our sects have powerful political representation in the Western countries where Israel always needs to maintain good relations.

"Whenever the Christian community asks for something, the authorities always comply. But then they always manage to remind the Christians how little they did for the Jews when the Jordanians were in charge here. It's true, of course," he admits ruefully with a nod of the head, "but they have this guilt thing....

"We — the Roman Church, I mean, will always be here," continues Father Michael. "Everybody else will run out of money long before the Vatican. Take the Greeks and the Armenians; without American millions they'd have sold their buildings and left long ago."

The Municipality is also confronted with such blunt fiscal truths. Despite its national and international status, the Jerusalem government is well-known for being handicapped with uniquely limited powers. Take, for example, electricity problems; Jerusalem's creaking infrastructure makes for plenty of such crises over the hot summers. "There's probably no other mayor in the world who is so personally harassed by his citizens because of cuts in electricity," notes Amir Cheshin. "No matter that the electric services have nothing to do with the city, that they are different companies, run by a different system.

"Whenever there are electrical cutbacks on the east side of the city, they call me, they call Teddy, to complain," he continues. "As though we had the means to fix the service ourselves! The East Jerusalem company is a local Jordanian company, while West Jerusalem and the rest of the country are supplied by the national company. The people have no idea how many things the Municipality does not control!"

So if Teddy cannot control, he influences," explains restauranteur Gershon Rubin. "Officially Teddy's people are forbidden to have any talks with Palestinians who might have the slightest possible connection with the PLO, which is like saying you can't talk to any Catholic who has connections with the Pope," Rubin notes with a shrug. "But he has ways of dealing with things."

Where control ends, influence begins, but contact must be very carefully made. Recently four Israelis received six-month prison sentences for violation of the Prevention of Terror Law, which outlaws any contact with organizations outlawed by the State. Obviously there has to be contact with Palestinian organizations; the pragmatics of running a city override political emotions. "If we have a problem concerning the merchants, we discuss it with the East Jerusalem Chamber of Commerce. From time to time we can find a common word with them," observes Amir Cheshin. "We never *officially* discuss politics with editors of East Jerusalem papers. Unofficially we do it on an individual basis; but never officially. We have no mandate to discuss politics, nevertheless politics is part of our lives. So we are always ready to sit down with Palestinians to discuss anything. We simply must talk to these people with whom we will have to live the rest of our lives."

Oftimes, especially in delicate situations, it serves the Municipality's best interests to stand apart from the national government. "Since the reunification of '67, Teddy's office has to manage new settlement villages within Municipal boundaries," notes Gershon Rubin. "Look, most of the land for new districts like Ramot, Neve Ya'akov, Gilo and Talpiot was forcibly confiscated from Arabs. The government did it and left Teddy to manage it all," Rubin comments with a note of irony. "Some people have even said that is why the intifada has been successful here, but I think that is not so true."

These are places where tensions run high, and the Jerusalem Foundation, too, is caught in between. "It's easy to find a donor for a community center in Gilo or Neve Ya'akov," notes Barri Avnerre. "But when you look at the poorer Arab neighborhoods nearby, the contrast is all the more irritating for those Arabs."

By comparison, Foundation renovations to the house of Rabbi Mordechai Weingarten have turned it into the Old Yishuv Court Museum, a vivid collection of restored memorabilia from the pre-1948 period of life in the Jewish Quarter. Contemplate the memorial built out of the ruins of the Hurva Synagogue, and the bitter words of East Jerusalem attorney Achmed Madlaj take on additional ironies: "The Jews spend millions to change old ruins where nobody lives into new ruins where nobody lives. They spend money on monuments before they build houses and schools. Please, my friend, think about how much money the Palestinians save just by living in *unimproved* ruins!"

The shoe is also on the other foot; in East Jerusalem Arabs live on land that was purchased by the Jewish National Fund, as Amir Cheshin describes. "Before 1948 Arabs sold land to Jews. At those times every square inch of Jewish land was bought, not confiscated, from the Arabs with money from the Jewish National Fund. Even today there are places in Silwan where Arabs live in houses originally purchased by the Jewish National Fund in the '20s and '30s. They're still registered under the name of the JNF even though only Arabs live there now."

"Listen, my friend," Khalil Naihmi confides, "in the Middle East, ownership of the land is the big issue. I am sorry Teddy Kollek must govern after the troubles caused by the government. Many, many times they have moved out our people, always against their wishes, to make room for new Jewish villages. In 1948 they machine gunned our people at Deir Yassin; Meir Kahane has firebombed Palestinians out from Neve Ya'acov; their bulldozers have torn up our olive trees. For years there are situations which cry out for justice. It is unfortunate that only a few people understand why Teddy cannot always make immediate cures. Here there is a very delicate political balance. When things are wrong, people wish for action immediately, but many times it is more correct to do nothing for the moment so that bad feelings may not be made worse."

What happens after Kollek? "For 21 years Teddy Kollek has been keeping the peace mostly by talking and dealing," notes Gershon Rubin, neatly summing up the mayor's *modus operandi*. "Now that he's 77, his clock shows just the littlest sign of winding down. But only a little," he is quick to add.

"The problem is who will come after him. Like many great men, he thinks he will live forever, so he has not cultivated a successor. But, you understand, anyone big enough to fill Kollek's boots would have such *chutzpah* himself that he could never work under Teddy long enough to get experience for the job."

This is Jerusalem, after all, so the eventual solution will not be a simple one.... ∎

60

OPPOSITE: Looking west from the Mt. of Olives at the Old City, past the Mary Magdalene Church to the Dome of the Rock. ABOVE: During Passover celebrations Orthodox Jews dance in front of the Western Wall; a Palestinian falafel maker just inside Damascus gate.

*An Iraqi rabbi near the Western Wall, preparing to blow his shofar during Passover celebrations.*

*A Haredi praying at the Western Wall. Innumerable written supplications are crammed into every available crevice; an Orthodox rabbi lays tfflin during a Bar Mitzvah at the Western Wall; reading from the Torah at Passover.*

64

ARISE, SHINE OUT

*Bible and rosary during prayers in the Church of the Holy Sepulchre.*

*Pilgrims celebrate mass inside the Church of the Holy Sepulchre; an Orthodox procession on Palm Sunday; an Orthodox priest reads the Bible by candle light.*

ARISE, SHINE OUT

*The Russian Orthodox Church of Mary Magdalene on the Mount of Olives; the Citadel at night. David's tower near the Jaffa Gate, dates back to Herod around 24 BCE.*

*The magnificent Dome of the Rock in Haram esh-Sharif, "the noble sanctuary," one of the most important shrines in Islam.*

*Intricate tiling covering the Dome of the Rock. This impressive work dates back to the Ottoman Sultan Suleiman the Magnificent of the sixteenth century; Muslim faithful making ablutions at El Kas purification fountain.*

*A cobblesone
street leading to
the entrance of the
Mosque of Omar.*

*A soldier on duty in the Old City.*

*A young vegetable seller in the bustling Damascus Gate market; a boy delivers bread on Paratrooper Street; colorful clothing on display in the Muslim Quarter of the Old City.*

A bird's eye view of Ben Yehuda Street mall at night; a couple enjoys sharing falafel; a few young people enjoy themselves outside one of the many cafes. Much of Jerusalem night life can be found on Ben Yehuda Street.

*Ramot, a suburb of western Jerusalem. These uniquely shaped houses form separate clusters on the hill tops.*

*The rebuilt Jewish Quarter of the Old City illuminated at night; Silwan village by moonlight; Center city at dawn.*

*The Hurva Synagogue.*

*The Shrine of the Book.*

The Monument of the Fallen at Yad Vashem commemorates Jewish soldiers who fell in the war against National Socialism. RIGHT: A Holocaust memorial at Yad Vashem depicts the Polish teacher Janusz Korczak who voluntarily accompanied his orphan students to the death camp at Treblinka.

*The poignancy of Memorial Day — at the military cemetery on Mt. Herzl.*

ABOVE: The exhuberant revelry of Independence
Day begins at sunset with the sounding of a
siren signifying the end of Memorial Day. This
dicotomy of emotions is uniquely Israeli.
RIGHT: Fireworks above the Old City wall
on Jerusalem Day, May 15th.

*Fern-covered grotto at Ein Gedi Nature Reserve.*

# REBUILT BY THE LAND

"WE CAME TO BUILD THE LAND, AND to be rebuilt by it," went a familiar Zionist folk song, joyously hummed by the early settlers of Israel. And since the time of the first *aliyah* to the establishment of the State of Israel 40 years ago, the Land of Zion has developed from a backwater of the Ottoman Empire to a fully-modernized participant in the First World.

Israel "is the land in which our fathers have found rest since time immemorial — and as they lived so shall we live," wrote Zionist poet Moshe Lilienblum. "Let us go now into the only land in which we will find relief for our souls that have been harassed by murderers for these thousands of years. Our beginnings will be small, but in the end we will flourish."

The land held many things for the Diaspora: a record of their past in the times of Isaiah and King David, as well as the key to the future of the Jewish people. Now once again the ancient homeland would become the cultural and spiritual center for the Jewish nation. When the 19th Century Zionists first dreamed of Eretz Yisrael, the actual land of Palestine was a hostile place, geographically and culturally. With little more than crumbled ruins of times long gone to offer, the land of Israel was settled and developed. Cities were built, crops and forests were planted, roads were paved and Israel became a First World country amidst a sea of Third World neighbors. But what of preserving the natural wonders in this diverse land — a land of snowy mountains, rolling hills and lush meadows, of crackling hot deserts, Sienna-colored mesas and barren plains? On the verge of being overpaved, overgrazed and overused, great measures have had to be taken to preserve the environment so that people, nature and history can coexist peacefully.

**P**erhaps with no other culture does history play so important a role. No sooner was the dream of a Jewish homeland launched by the "Chovevei Zionists" than land was purchased and archaeologists set to laying a claim to their ancestral homeland. Not only did they uncover their own past, but the histories of the many and varied other peoples who had inhabited this crossroads of three continents for more than 50 centuries, from the Phoenicians and Philistines to the Romans and Turks.

Professor Benjamin Mazar of Hebrew University was one of the first Israeli archaeologists to make great discoveries. Two of his most notable digs are a Philistine settlement on Tel Qasila, near the river Yarkon in Tel Aviv; and Bet She'arim, where catacombs from soon after the time of the Bar Kochba revolt of 132-135 BCE were discovered. He recalls the early years of archaeology in Israel. "From the time of my first dig with Albright in 1931 and the establishment of the State of Israel, archaeology has become an important element in the life of the country.

"But when we first started excavating, people didn't understand, and were not very helpful. We had many problems with organization and how to excavate. In 1936, my brother-in-law, who was the president of the State, received a message from one of the first settlers in the area of Bet She'arim, saying there were things of interest in the area with many inscriptions. Immediately we decided to go and see it, but had no idea how we would get there. We had no car.

"So we went to the American School and Dr. Macowen brought us to the site. We spent from 3 PM to 6 AM investigating, and decided that it was a site of major importance which had to be excavated. Our first question was 'How do we do it?' because this was the moment when the disturbances between Jews and Arabs had started. The second was where to get the money to finance the project and the people to do it. We ended up using members of a new kibbutz, who were involved in the excavation from 1936-40.

"In 1948 we were excavating Tel Qasila in Tel Aviv during the War of Independence," Mazar continues. "But we had no problems — the soldiers were even helping us to work because it was important for the new State. This was the beginning. Development was tremendous at first, but it was very hard to find Israeli archaeologists. The new universities (the Technion and

Hebrew University) helped with the great discoveries in Jerusalem.

"But it was [former IDF Chief-of-Staff] Yigael Yadin with his discovery of Masada who gave a tremendous push to Israeli archaeology. He was great at public relations — a genius, the greatest genius in public relations as well as with excavations. First of all he published lists to give it international importance, and secondly, he made everything grandiose. Later all the youngsters heard the stories of Yadin's excavations, and they are still repeating them. This is what made him great. This was the turning point in Israeli archaeology."

Much has changed from the early days of having to borrow a car to get to a site of major importance. "Archaeology today does not compare with the archaeology of 50 years ago because of many different reasons," Mazar expounds. "New methods of technology, facilities and organizations make it easier, as well as the development of relations between archaeologists here and institutions abroad through joint efforts. This is something new: all the work is done together and we are therefore able to find more funds and people. Every discussion is international.

"Archaeology is popular, and this is good," muses Mazar. "Sometimes it is bad when people who don't understand are involved just because of business or public relations. And the fanatics who oppose excavations, who jump into the graves saying we are desecrating Jewish remains — they are fanatics! But really they are not so important. The important thing is that archaeology is now a part of the country. It was at first limited to a few sites and a few people.

"From my point of view, what happened to archaeology is what happened to the Bible. In the beginning the Bible was limited to a certain group of persons who understood it, not the entire people. Now it is all over the world. It's not comparable, but it is more or less the same idea."

Kurt Raveh, a marine archaeologist from Tel Dor, concurs that Israeli archaeology is indeed becoming more international.

"Whatever project there is in Israel, you need funding from abroad — today from the States. I play this very clever. Usually the institutions get so wrapped up in the bureaucracy, that the archaeology of the academic world and things like that cost a lot and actually produce very little. Most of our colleagues have worked for many years finding a few stones, then they write beautiful articles that only their mothers read. Their other colleagues generally disagree with their findings anyway. At Tel Dor we made our own company; we are a trust. We have our own team here which works well in archaeology and also in the tourist field.

"We bring our information straight to the people," notes Raveh, "and the finances from the tourism also keeps the academic work going so we don't have to use the taxpayers' money. So without being smothered to death by all the bureaucratic things, we have our field that we work freely."

Excavations at Tel Dor have uncovered the remains of an important Phoenician port city. The Phoenicians inhabited the Tel Dor area for over 1,000 years, coexisting at various times with Egyptians, Greeks, Romans and Israelites. Underwater archaeology at Tel Dor is extremely extensive; 90% of the artifacts are recovered from depths of less than five meters. The oldest finds are Canaanite artifacts, while the most recent are bronze cannons thrown overboard during Napoleon's retreat from Lebanon in 1798. Tel Dor is an active dig during the summer months, and over 40 students assist with the work. Each shard is meticulously recorded because, as Raveh states, "pottery is the calendar of the history of the Holy Land. In Egypt — where they have wall paintings, pictures, tombs and millions of artifacts —they dump out pots like this. Here it's most important because the land has been the bridge between three continents. Israel has been rocked and destroyed for strategic reasons or religious reasons or whatever reasons for centuries, so there is very little left. We are very careful in our procedures, and we account for every bit of pottery excavated in the dig. Otherwise you get like Bet Shean, where the object is not creating new scientific work, but building a tourist site."

Although effort is made to open the ancient sites to the public, great concern is voiced over the wisdom of this decision. "The tourists and people of Israel who visit these important sites seem to have little or no regard for them. Just look at the litter and graffiti all over," exclaims a young man from Tel Aviv. "In order to make the State of Israel great, we must appreciate our past and what resources we have been given by God."

Kurt Raveh has mixed emotions about the issue. "A common phrase here is 'the stones gave something to the people.' I get very mixed feelings sometimes because archaeology is always destruction, and we are all guilty of this. Archaeology is a small society, and most of the finds are put in a storeroom or scientific libraries so a lot of this information never gets to the people. This is why many people feel 'who needs it?' about archaeology. They are alienated from it, not connected and thinking that it is only for tourists.

"Bet Shean will be a fantastic site for people who don't know archaeology. They are now using bulldozers there! But I am afraid, personally, that there is not enough money. The problem is already there. They have no one who will be there to preserve the site well, and all the beauty that is being uncovered at the moment will be soon gone. The local townspeople oftentimes continue the excavations to create their own private museums after the workers have gone home. For me archaeology is like a dream, but it is also a problem because it is easy for people to steal things."

Lawrence Stager, an American professor from Harvard University, is the supervisor of an excavation at Ashkelon, where the tel is an important archaeological site. "What is most unique and exciting about the work being conducted at Ashkelon is the chronicling and piecing together of the histories of so many cultures," notes Stager. "Seven different civilizations have existed there over history: Philistines, Canaanites, Greeks, Byzantine Christians, Romans, Mamelukes and Crusaders. We do a lot of discussing and debating, almost like a seminar. It's more stimulating than any project on which I have worked to-date, and one of the more complicated sites ever excavated.

"In fact, the British excavated at Ashkelon in 1920-1. After digging for two years and reaching nothing earlier than the Hellenistic period, Professor John Garstang got frustrated and gave up the project.

"Of all the coastal cities south of Jaffa, Ashkelon is the only port that sits right on the sea, occupying one of the few coastal conjunctions where fertile soil, sweet ground water and the Mediterranean Sea provide an economy based on agriculture, commerce and maritime activity. In addition to commerce, one of the foci of our excavation is to research the variety of peoples and ethnicities that populated this bustling port and left behind their collective identities amid the rubble of the tel.

"Ashkelon was the major commercial center for the area and a port of international significance. Goods from far off places such as Egypt, Carthage, Spain, Italy, Crete and the Aegean were reaching the port and making their way to the civilizations in the highlands. Through a complex trading network, Philistine goods could reach the hills and Israelite produce the coast without the two groups ever making face-to-face contact," Stager remarks.

"A few of the most fascinating finds we have had — and with which American newspapers have had a heyday — are a dog cemetery dating from the time of Persian rule, about 500-450 BCE, and the remains of a Roman bath house/brothel. We call the dog burial site a 'mystery in progress.' Over 50 complete dog skeletons, including puppies, were found at the site, each buried on its side. No grave goods were found associated with these burials, so we are not exactly sure of their purpose. It's still an enigma.

"The *New York Post* got quite a charge out of the discovery of the bath house from the Late Roman period. The most prominent feature was a plaster-lined tub with three steps leading down to it. The pool was originally covered with a canopy supported with four heart-shaped columns. On the curtain wall of the pool was a Greek inscription translated as 'Enter in, Enjoy, and...' Pieces of erotic art were also discovered nearby. The *Post* titled their article 'Profs Dig Ancient Sin City Sex Den.' It makes me glad that I made a contribution to science!"

Joking aside, Stager shares the concerns of Kurt Raveh about the preservation of these ancient sites. His budget includes funds for the landscaping and restoration of the Byzantine Church of St. Mary of the Green, as soon as there is some guarantee of maintenance by park authorities.

Unavoidably, riddles and questions abound in the study of archaeology: 'Who came first,' 'Who did what to whom,' and 'Are we destroying the past in order to know it?' On balance, most Israelis seem to think it's worth the risk.

Archaeological finds at Masada, Bet She'arim and others like them confirm the Jewish history writers like Flavius Josephus recorded nearly two millennia ago. The return to Eretz Yisrael after a long absence was to be accompanied by the fulfillment of the Jewish spirit. In his 1907 essay *Some Observances*, A.D. Gordon wrote "...Our people can be rejuvenated only if each one of us recreates himself through labor and a life close to nature." Poet Micah Joseph Lebensohn described Israel as "the land where the muses dwell, where each flower is a psalm, each cedar a song divine, each stone a book and each rock a tablet." Yet the pioneers were astounded by the reality of the grueling hours of hard labor, as well as the many illnesses that plagued them. But with grim determination the people of the first and second *aliyot* harvested the land many had thought uncultivable.

"I would say the success of agricultural development has its roots in the strong desire to return to the land," comments Professor Amram Ashri of the Faculty of Agriculture, Hebrew University. "Returning to the land means not only to the land of Zion, but to till the soil. One of the most important aspects before the state was established was to conquer the land and make it bloom. They said, 'it can't be done, the land is poor, the soil is poor and it will be difficult. It is hot in the summer and there is no water' and so on. The idea was to return and apply the newest technology of science to this land that had been depleted over many generations, overgrazed for thousands of years, cultivated one way or another and destroyed by terrorists," recalls Professor Ashri.

"To do so we had to go through a phase when agriculture was not easy, with a lot of trials and errors; you grew this, you grew that. But through this we accumulated a lot of knowledge for our own research. From the beginning agriculture was to have a high priority on the national scale, because returning to till the land was important."

Because Israel is the homeland for the Jewish nation," says Jewish National Fund spokesperson David Angel, "the JNF was created to enable the Jewish people to own the land after two thousand years of absence from the area. It is our mandate to implement this operation with the funds allocated by the Jewish people of the world.

"In the '20s and '30s the JNF redeemed hundreds of thousands of dunams of land which was not where everyone wanted to settle. The land the JNF bought in that period was swamps all over in the Jezre'el and the areas between Hadera and Netanya. The land was swampy because the people didn't know how to technically cope with an underground aquifer that comes to the surface. The local Arab Sheik could do nothing with it, so he was more than happy to sell it. The JNF was instrumental in the draining of the Hula swamp, which is now a very fertile agricultural area. We are always experimenting and trying new things. That's the challenge for 40 years of day-to-day work."

The mandate of the JNF is not without its problems, Angel points out. "If we would like to secure the homeland for the entire Jewish nation, the actual land that we have is not able to absorb them since over 65% of the nation is the Negev Desert. We accept it that God gave Israel this desert. Some other nations would take it as a curse; we take it as a blessing. There are two kinds of desert: the kind that you think is all arid unless you water it, and the physical desert that you try to push back. We believe, as Ben-Gurion said, that He wanted to make us partners in the process of creation. So wherever we can plant forests, we plant forests; wherever we can create agricultural land, we create agricultural land," he notes with enthusiasm.

"We don't only work on afforestation, we also work on land development. It's not enough to be the owner of the land; if you don't use the land, if you don't develop the land, you don't control the land. The real owner of the land is the one who tills the land and lives on it," opines Angel. "Our goal is to afforestate 5% of all Israel. The planter tree population is now over 180 million trees. Our dream, which was Ben-Gurion's vision, is 500 million trees."

The JNF has projects building national recreation parks and forests all over the country, most notably the Peace Forest near Sinai and the Balfour Forest in the Galil. "One third of our efforts is concentrated in the Negev," Angel expounds. "We are in the process of creating a greenbelt around Beersheba which will take about 20 years, so it will be for our children and grandchildren. All around the Negev we have afforestation projects which are mainly next to the highways, where we use the waters that have collected from the rains. We call them 'liman', or mini-oasis; in Greek it means 'port.' Along the Arava highway the JNF has created agricultural land where we use a very special technology of bringing in earth, washing it, then maintaining it very carefully because the land is very saline."

In the arid land of Israel, careful management of reclaimed desert is imperative, a fact not lost on one of the Negev's biggest promoters, Israel's first Prime Minister David Ben-Gurion. He once said, "if the State does not put an end to the desert, the desert may put an end to the State." Nowhere else on earth are agronomists so mindful of his prophetic words.

Professor Amos Richmond, the first chairman of the Jacob Blaustein Institute for Desert Research in Sde Boker, claims that "humanity will rediscover that the arid lands, the deserts, are actually very good places to live. It's just a problem of learning how to live there, not just simply copying systems whether it be house building or agriculture from temperate zones.

"What is needed is to develop arid zone civilization, technology, agriculture, philosophy. Then many dry areas in the world will be good places to live and prosper. I have little doubt that this is what is going to happen, but it will take a lot more research."

Desert Research architect Isaac "Saki" Meyer agrees. "I think that [settlement in the desert] is imperative. Because, if I am limiting myself only to Israel, the Negev is 65% of the area of the country inside the 1967 borders. Today it is settled by under 6% of the population, which makes it very sparsely populated. From the climatic point of view, I believe the Negev has some of the advantages of Israel because most of the areas are dry. Even if they are very hot, they are comfortable in the summertime. In wintertime they can be very cold, but this can be solved with passive solar designs."

"There are also security considerations. There are almost a million and a half out of our 3½ million population concentrated along the coastal zone, and this makes for quite a problem. This population could be easily dispersed in this no man's land. On the coast stress is an understatement. Tel Aviv is a real monster; if you try to drive you car in there, it's awful!"

"People are wary of coming to the desert," comments Meyer. "It's not only the isolation, but people also have a very distorted perception of the desert. For instance, I am from Greece. I was born there, and until I came to the Negev in 1980 I had been living in Israel for already six years. My picture of the desert was something like Lawrence of Arabia, with sand dunes and Bedouin on camels shouting 'Aqaba! Aqaba!'

"It is nothing like that. People think that it is very hot here, but our problem is mostly the cold. People also think that it's hot 24 hours a day, but summer nights are pretty cool here. You sit outside and you need a sweater or something.

"Isolation is a real problem. It has nothing to do with psychological bias, and I don't see how this can be solved until the desert starts becoming fairly populated."

"If we really want to become members of the desert, we have to understand the desert laws," counsels Moshe Shackak, ecologist at the Desert Research Institute. "If you don't understand the desert laws, you won't know what to do. I came to the desert 20 years ago, and you might say I fell in love with it mentally because I wanted to understand the processes here. I have been studying desert ecology for many years, and every day I know less. Now I know that I am leaving a few questions for my grandson!" he laughs.

"You see, it's a very complex thing. So little rain, very few animals, very little human activities. With our small brains we will understand it after a while. I believe we can do a lot here for human benefit, for nature conservation and for just having this area as real desert for tourism.

"The solution for the State of Israel is to build cities in the desert," continues Shackak. "It is very important to know how to do it, especially for a State like Israel where we have no other empty places to build our country. If I am right in my opinion, we have to produce two solutions: how to convert 5% of the desert to non-desert, and secondly, what to do with the remaining 95% of the land. This, as with most processes, has both its costs and benefits.

"Man is now able with high technology to overcome what is the big problem of the desert: water. For water you need only a pipe. Now for the climate. We have solar housing and that's beautiful. It's very nice to live here, no problem at all."

Meyer agrees with his colleague Shackak, "It depends on the type of settlements you would be employing. If one uses the traditional type of settlement, you need a lot of energy and water input. We are going towards a more alternative way of designing self-supporting settlements which can supply themselves from a water and energy point of view. Also maybe food. One can build an almost limitless number of them. Naturally one has to take into consideration the ecological aspects, because most of the ecosystems in the desert are very delicately balanced. If one comes into the desert with a very western-oriented mind, one can really destroy what is going on," warns Meyer.

Since early days, settlement of immigrants has been a function of the Jewish Agency; oftimes the Agency's plans for new arrivals were based on government needs and did not coincide with the desires of the new *olim*. Today all areas of Israel require important decisions; not only cultural and ecological ones, but political considerations as well.

Eli Kubesi of the Jewish Agency Settlements Division comments, "to date there are 1,056 settlements with about 75,000 people living in them. Since 1977 you can see a change. That is the year the Likud came into power, and since then there have been 259 settlements built behind the Green Line. We are also building in the Galil and the Negev.

"In Israel settling is working with movements; movements belong to parties and parties are politics. The ideology of the Likud Party does not differentiate between the old boundaries and east of the Green line, before '67 and after '67. All parts of Israel are equal for them. There is a difference with the Labour Party. They prefer, for example, to build in the Galil and the Arava rather than in Judea and Samaria or on the Jordan border. Their ideology says one day you will have to give back those areas," explains Kubesi.

"We feel that you might have to compromise in several areas, and give back those areas to the PLO or to the Federation of Jordan," he adds.

"When we establish a settlement, first we have to identify that the area does not belong to the King of Jordan or to the State, and is not private property. When we have identified this land that doesn't belong to anybody, we can start building the settlement. Sometimes we find that even if the land belongs to the King or to the State, some people have already planted some trees there, usually olive trees, and we don't touch it. When somebody has planted something it is very hard to take back the land. Under Ottoman law that person has a 'hold' on the land even though he doesn't own it."

As for people who will live on the settlements, Kubesi explains, "there are many procedures which go into selecting people for the settlements. First, settlements belong to movements approved by the Agency. Most people who are going to these areas go either for ideology or ecology. They want to get out of Tel Aviv or out of the cities, out of the pollution or whatever. Or they want a place where they can build a house and have a nice garden and all their neighbors can have the same. To be a settler means you need special qualities to live in this kind of settlement. Most of the time they are living in small groups of 30, 40 or 50 families — this is not big, it is not a town.

"Usually in the settlements that we build, we bring our own industry or high-tech, computers and so on. Most of the people in these settlements are above average, so they can work in high-tech. Now we are trying to bring more industry — private and public —and tourism into the areas of Judea and Samaria."

Kubesi concedes that settlement location is still often a function of government need. "Usually we go and find places that are needed strategically for the State. For example, if there are two or three settlements up in the hills and close to one another, we have to close that circle. Our priority has been in Judea and Samaria over the last few years. Only two settlements have been formed in the Golan Heights in that time. In the Golan there is already Israeli law, so there is no rush to settle there. It is more important to go and fix things in other places. Especially if you want to take a hold in these areas so that you can bargain later in negotiations.

"For instance in Jerusalem, I would like to see a chain of settlements around the city. Jerusalem is a big metropolitan area, and there is a diffusion of Arab settlements around and inside Jerusalem. Villages are growing fast. They get money and they build through their organizations. They have money from Saudi Arabia and from the PLO, also from their agents in Europe and from charity organizations. There are ways to bring it in, so they build fast around there. So that's exactly what we need now, especially in the eastern quarters of Jerusalem."

If geopolitics aren't on everyone's mind, certainly the Jewish Agency is sensitive to the territorial designs of the Likud and those of like philosophy. "It's a race to settle in the administered areas," Kubesi admits. "From the old Green Line to the sea is only 15 km. We can never have the border there again because in half an hour enemy forces could cut Israel into two pieces. We are building a chain of settlements, and we put trees between the cities to hold the area.

"We call it a 'hot dog'; this way they cannot come in and cut. If you want to bargain in the future for a real border, this security border is the only way you can do it. Otherwise you get back to the '67 line which I don't believe will bring peace. This stimulates war. When you have problems with a neighbor and you want to fight, and you know that he has only a little bit and you can cut it, this stimulates you to do it.

"One of the theses in politics is that conditions bring peace or war. Conditions inside the country and outside the country. Let's say some people here and there could sit and talk at the table one day: I try to fix facts, they try to fix facts. I think the whole area will be under negotiations in the future. Any side would like to secure itself. As for me, as for the way I see it, Palestinians have no reason to secure themselves because they could never start wars. We will never attack just to be an instigator, but we will have to secure ourselves. I'm not talking about the '48 war, the British Mandate taking land from us and so on. We are talking only about '67 and the situation of '67 cannot return. If this is returned, this is bringing us to the destroying of Israel."

Rabbi Menachem Fruman, a Gush Emunim settler from Tekoa, admits that settling in the West Bank is indeed a controversial issue. "The Zionist idea is settling the land of Israel, and that includes the West Bank and the Gaza Strip. It is impossible that a Jew will renounce Judea. Remember, in Hebrew, Jew=Yehudi, Judea=Yehuda. Giving up the West Bank will not bring spiritual profit any more than the contribution of the Jews to the Communist Revolution in Russia in 1917." An unusual parallel, perhaps, but nevertheless it's a common sentiment in the West Bank.

The problems of settling the territories and maintaining security are not new. From the very first kibbutzim established in the Galil to the Gush Emunim settlements in the West Bank, security is a major issue. Even today it is not unusual to see barbed wire surrounding a kibbutz, with a special guard gate, gun turrets and bomb shelters from days past. Indeed it is a national law which requires every village to have bomb shelters sufficient for all the inhabitants. Although most are painted in bright colors and serve as young people's recreation rooms, they are sad reminders that a state of war still exists with Arab neighbors. Particularly in the northern areas, the threat of attack by hostile neighbors or the frequent incursions by terrorists produce a state of emergency constantly reinforced by the presence of the military. Hulks of tanks, 20 year-old minefields, shrapnel-punctured ruins are omnipresent remains of bygone battles with invading neighbors.

From his kibbutz less than a kilometer from Gaza, Bini Shafrir explains, "when I first joined Nahal Oz in 1936, I was part of the special army unit, 'Nahal,' which is an acronym in Hebrew for 'Fighting Pioneer Youth.' The Nahal units established many of the kibbutzim in the early days of the State, and Nahal Oz was the first. Our primary concerns were agriculture and security; we used to work in the fields near the border with at least one armed guard securing the workers. At night we needed two guards. Although there was always some kind of army unit in the area, the IDF never helped us to secure the kibbutz. That was our job, along with the workers in the field.

"At that time, there were a lot of things that the Arabs from the Gaza Strip used to do to us. Because at those times there was no barbed-wire fence at the border, there was no problem crossing it," recalls Shafrir. "They used to lay mines on the dirt roads where the tractors would drive to work. They used to force their sheep and goat herds on the crop fields; when it was dry, they used to set the fields on fire."

Rafael Lanzer of Kibbutz Nof Ginossar remembers the security provisions in the establishment of his kibbutz. "We erected not only tents and houses, we erected a whole camp with a watch tower in the mid-dle of it, a wall around it and a double wall inside. Between the walls we put stones and sand so the wall became bullet-proof.

"During that period there were Arab terrorist groups. Their leader was the famous Mufti of Jerusalem who was a supporter of Hilter during World War II. These terrorist groups attacked mostly at nighttime. That is why we had our searchlight up in the watchtower. The view from the lakeside perhaps reminded me of an American fort against the Indians. We lived like this for more than two years, and only after 1939 did we start building the first houses outside the walls."

Not only was maintaining security difficult, but the actual development of the land took incredible stamina. "At that time we didn't have tractors; all the work had to be done by hand," Lanzer recalls. "We had groups all over the country to earn money for the settler group that remained here and prepared the land, removing stones and thorn bushes. It took us years and years; you couldn't live off the land in the early times."

These days life at Kibbutz Nof Ginossar is very different. "Today, our houses hold two families. Today I can say we live in above-normal conditions; our apartments have air conditioning, we have two rooms and a kitchen with a Frigidaire and gas so you may do some cooking if you want to. There is a budget for furniture so that you may buy to your tastes. We have telephone and color TV at home. As I said, it's more or less normal standard. You will find that in many kibbutzim they will build two additional rooms, and there the children sleep all the time with their parents."

Today many of the kibbutzim have branched out into industry to make up for the lack of resources, as well as attract new members with talents other than purely agricultural. On the whole, kibbutz industries have been successful ventures, ranging from injection moulding plastics to owning and operating container ships. They have also been instrumental in promoting new technology, particularly in the desert areas.

"We came here and settled, but now there is no more land. That means we can't grow additional crops, so each kibbutz must start new work, usually in industry.

"One of our biggest problems is how to keep the young people with us. I would even say that one of the reasons that we started with industry in the kibbutzim is to give people the opportunity to study not only agriculture but other professions. Each kibbutz is interested in growing and accepting new members, not all of them farmers. The land in Israel is already very limited," notes Lanzer.

"I haven't the faintest notion as to whether this nation would have developed without the Kibbutz movement," ponders Professor Yoash Vaadia, Vice President of Hebrew University. "Israeli society didn't start because of the Kibbutz Movement, and I don't think it has survived because of it. It was an uncontrolled experiment and a way to allow a large number of people to settle at a relatively low cost. If not for the Kibbutz movement, the country wouldn't have managed to absorb and settle so many people from the outside. There wouldn't have been such an impact on the development of the language, or on the ecological development of the economy. I think everything would have happened, but at a slower rate."

Most people would equate development with progress, but in Israel too rapid development has placed undue stress on the environment. In this small country of 4 million people, with limited land and limited resources, the 'empty' wild lands are subjected to intense pressures by development and industrial projects, as well as the land requirements of various government agencies such as the army.

"The founding fathers of the State of Israel, having to house a mass immigration of Holocaust survivors and Jewish refugees from Arab countries in a land much neglected over the centuries, elevated the slogan 'Make the Desert Bloom' to a national ideology," writes Joseph Shadur of the Society for Protection of Nature in Israel. "Popular songs extolled the virtues of building: 'Oh our country, we will dress you in cement and asphalt....'

"The desert and empty spaces were the ultimate challenge to the generation of state-builders, the 'conquest' of the desert their chief mission. Who, in those days, gave any thought to the ecological effects of rapid building on the landscape or the wild animals and plants of the country? How does one change such ingrained habits — especially when it means bucking a fundamental creed of one's society?" queries Shadur.

The landscape was not the only thing endangered by the rapid development of the land. According to Giora Ilani of the Nature Reserve Authority, "since Biblical times, the wildlife of Israel has dwindled either in special composition or in quantity of populations. Lion, bear, hippopotamus, red dear, roe deer, wild ass, white oryx, wild goat, ostrich and cheetah had all become extinct through the ages. When Israel won its independence, a mere handful of game species still inhabited remote areas, at very low population levels: two gazelle species, the Nubian ibex, wild boar, were notable herbivores. Of the carnivores, only the caracal cat, the wolf, the striped hyena and the leopard, survived the long extermination process."

"At one time we had wolves in Israel," jokes Ra'anan Boral, the SPNI Field School Director at Ein Gedi. "But their territories are so large that if an entire pack were to live here now and evolve, there wouldn't be any room left for the Jews or the Palestinians!"

It was not until 1953, when a group of teachers and scientists got together to protest the draining of the Hula swamplands, that any action was taken to preserve the special, delicate environment of Israel. "When we started the Society for the Protection of Nature in Israel (SPNI) in 1953," continues Boral, "no one knew about us. Today, the SPNI has over 45,000 members and everybody knows what the SPNI is. It's like a private company that belongs to the public. First, the SPNI was just the field schools where we wanted to educate the public about nature. Now the SPNI is invited to different committees for its input — the government is actually afraid of the Society! We have taken them to court and regional councils. As in most countries, the main lawbreaker is the governnment.

"In the 35 years that the SPNI has existed, so many things have changed. The projects don't always have something to do with nature alone, but also with the quality of the surroundings — the environment. Many of these projects are carried out through the SPNI now. The Nature Reserves Authority works with nature also, but it is a government body and, therefore, is to some extent limited in its battles against the government.

"Let's say the military wants to do something and the NRA is told not to oppose," hypothesizes Boral. "They cannot oppose. But we can take the government to court. Now if the military wants to build bases in a sensitive area, they call us. We have achieved a state where the military calls the rangers where before they never did. In fact, the military has been working in close cooperation with Yossi Leshem of the SPNI, mapping out bird migration routes. The planes avoid the areas through which the birds are migrating, and fewer accidents are caused by birds hitting the planes. Of course, this cooperation strengthens our authority."

From the beginning, practical work in nature conservation and the protection of the natural landscape involved educating the public," explains Yoav Sagi, former Secretary General of the SPNI. "We understood that protection of nature was impossible without awareness and general knowledge of our natural environment, and that this could only be fostered by field trips. Bringing the public into the countryside became the central work of the SPNI. The field trips and outings stimulated large numbers of people to deepen their attachment and involvement."

"As for our goals, in education we have been very successful," comments Ra'anan Boral. "At first all the money was spent on growth of the program, not on maintenance. Now they have stopped focusing on growth and are improving quality. The field school is the educational department of the SPNI, and subsidized by the Ministry of Education. In Ein Gedi, we have about 15 guides and six administrative workers. We organize different activities to reach different parts of the population. We have arrangements with the schools, and this gives the children the possibility to see and learn. It's like a museum without a roof."

Although the public is largely aware of the problems concerning the environment, their dedication to the issues is not always evident. Boral complains, "Our members number about 45,000 people in Israel. Mostly they come to the good things and are not really interested in the problems. They like to enjoy the beauty, but we don't know if we can always count on them. On various occasions we have had demonstrations where the numbers have reached up to 10,000 people. I don't think Israelis are that much involved; Israelis like to go out, but they don't really like to get involved in anything. Sometimes we fight something that would be really very convenient to have. Sometimes we have to oppose progress, at least in certain places, just to make sure that nature is represented.

"People had heard we were against the building of a road from the Dead Sea to Jerusalem that might jeopardize the environment. They were against us; they would like a more convenient road.

"Recently there was a movement opposing development near Ein Gedi. The developer had proposed to build a town of hotels for the tourist trade, but he had not even considered the impact on the environment. He worked on getting the things he needed, and we worked to prevent it. Water, for instance. He drilled and found good water. We were blockading then and told all the regional councils. Now everyone can get their share of that water. The builder claims we are prohibiting the development of the country. He said King Herod built his monument near here, and he wants to build *his*. It makes you wonder."

Conflicts will always be evident, and the fight will continue as to what is better for Israel or any state: development or preservation of natural resources. And Israelis, perhaps more than any people on Earth, are acutely aware of this scriptural warning: "When the Holy One, blessed be He, created the first man, He took him and warned him: 'See my works, how beautiful and perfect they are, and all I created, I created for you. Beware lest you spoil and destroy my world, for if you spoil it, there is no one to repair it after you.' " ■

Great Midrash on the Book of Ecclesiastes, Kohellet Rabba, 7.28

*The multi-hued sands of the Negev near Eilat.*

*From Eilat, Israel's toehold on the Red Sea, a sunrise view of the neighboring Jordanian city of Aqaba. The two cities coexist, sharing the harbor which is crucial to commerce in both nations; a sting ray on the bed of the Red Sea; a vibrantly colored coral cave. The Red Sea is home to many diverse lifeforms.*

102

OPPOSITE: Diving in
the Red Sea is a
popular pastime in
the vacation city,
Eilat; a giant
Napolean Wrasse
which can sometimes
weigh 2-400 pounds;
LEFT: Delicate rose
coral.

*ABOVE: The barren landscape of Timna, site of ancient
copper mines of the Egyptians in the 14th and 15th centuries
BCE. Mining was continued by King Solomon
and later by Israelis until 1976 when it proved unprofitable.
RIGHT: These beautifully patterned landscapes in the Negev
are the result of water and wind erosion. Although quite
picturesque, erosion is a serious problem in the desert
areas and much research is being done to find solutions.*

*ABOVE: An Oasis in the Arava with the Jordanian hills in the background; reintroduction of the ostrich originally started as part of the restoration of biblical wild life. Today Kibbutz Ha'on derives income from the valuable ostrich hide and feathers.*

*The Nubian ibex, the gecko, the bulbul, and the hyrax are now all present in the wild. The protection and reintroduction of many animals has been facilitated by the Nature Reserve Authority and the SPNI.*

REBUILT BY THE LAND

*Terrace on the west side of the Nabatean and Byzantine ruins of Avdat; arches in the residential quarter, dating from the Roman period. Archaeological sites appear at almost every turn in the road. Special measures are being taken to preserve the sites but much more needs to be done.*

REBUILT BY THE LAND

*ABOVE: Salt deposit formations in the Dead Sea, the saltiest and lowest lake in the world — at 400 meters below sea level. OPPOSITE: Sunrise from Masada; Dead Sea mud is said to have therapeutic qualities. People gather from all over the world to avail themselves of its healing powers; a bather enjoys the unique sensation of floating on the Dead Sea.*

REBUILT BY THE LAND

Erosion surrounds an abandoned Dead Sea Works mine. Erosion is quite a problem in the desert with its infrequent but intense rain showers; the Abatayim, or Chimney Cave, is formed by the erosion of salty soil near the Dead Sea.

*RIGHT: Nahal David
waterfall at Ein Gedi.
OPPOSITE: In an arid
country like Israel, the
people appreciate
water in all its
naturally occurring
forms and places.*

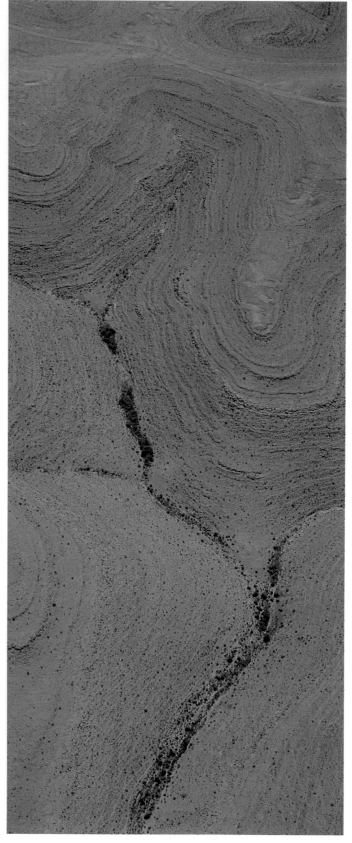

ISRAEL: IMAGES & IDEAS

*ABOVE: Frieze by the pool at Hisham's Palace, or Qirbat al-Mafyar, near Jericho. This summer palace was constructed in 724 by Hisham, the 10th Omayyad Khaliffa. It was never completed and was partly destroyed by an earthquake.*
*FAR LEFT: Wadi Qilt in the West Bank cuts through the hills of Judea down to the Plain of Jericho. The aqueduct built by Herod the Great provides water year 'round. The Greek Orthodox Monastery of St. George clings dramatically to the north face of the gorge.*
*LEFT: An aerial view of Wadi Qidron, south of Jericho.*

REBUILT BY THE LAND

ABOVE: Rugged coastline at Caesarea. The ruins of Herod's great port city nearby are being uncovered by teams of underwater archaeologists.
LEFT: Aerial view of Crusader walled moat at Caesarea, built in 1254 by Louis IX of France.
OPPOSITE: Crusader-era ruins near Ashdod.

RIGHT: Coastline cave at Rosh Hanikra, just south of the Lebanese border. BELOW:Brilliant algae colors the old natural breakwaters off the ancient port of Dor. Shallow pools in the rocks were used by the ancients to extract the valuable Tyrian purple dye from the murex snail.

120

Coastline at the ancient Phoenician port city of Dor, one of the greatest Levantine harbors before the construction of Caesarea. Natural breakwaters protected the harbor. Today Dor is the site of ongoing underwater and land excavations, revealing large quantities of important artifacts dating from Phoenician times through Napoleon's Wars.

*The highly cultivated Plain of Jezre'el. This fertile valley is the largest in Israel, separating the hills of Galilee and Samaria.*

LEFT: A view of the Jordan valley through an embrasure in the crusader fortress of Belvoir. The castle was built about 1130 on the destroyed site of Gerofina. Surrounded on three sides by huge moats the castle proved its strength by surviving an attack by Saladin.
BELOW: Discovered by a kibbutz member in 1936, Bet She'arim has been excavated since that time by archaeologists Benjamin Mazar and N. Avigad. Once a spiritual center for Jews after the failure of the Bar Kochba revolt, many pious Jews of ancient times are buried in the numerous catacombs.

OPPOSITE: A Greek Orthodox church at Capernaum; the sparkling Sea of Galilee.
LEFT: Looking down from a vantage point above cultivated kibbutz fields to the Sea of Galilee also called Lake Kinneret because it is shaped like a "kinneret" or "harp."

*Flowers of Israel which were once nearly picked to
extinction. The passage of the Protected Nature Value Laws
in the early '60s has saved not only Israel's wildflowers but
also many of its wild animals and unique ecological areas.*

REBUILT BY THE LAND

*ABOVE: Well protected borders serve as a reminder of Israel's close proximity to her less than friendly neighbors: Lebanon and Syria.*
*RIGHT: An old guard tower overlooks Kibbutz Nahal Oz, which officially became a Kibbutz in 1953. "Nahal" is an acronym for the "Pioneer Fighting Youth," and many kibbutzim were established by this special army unit. Nahal Oz is close to the Egyptian border and Gaza.*

*Near Tel Hai a bunker protectively overlooks farmland of Kfar Giladi that stretches north towards the Lebanese border. Many kibbutzim in the North are equipped with bunkers, watchtowers and shelters in case of invasion or terrorism. It was at Tel Hai that Josef Trumpeldor fell in 1921 defending the settlement from marauding Arabs. His dying words, "It is good to die for our country," made him a symbol for the new fighting Jew.*

REBUILT BY THE LAND

The Golan Heights, annexed by Israel from Syria in 1981, has a rugged, windblown beauty unlike any other area of Israel. Its strategic importance notwithstanding, the Golan is ripe for development in commerce, industry and settlement.
LEFT: A bullet-riddled mosque near Qazrin, inscribed with right-wing political graffiti.
BELOW: A Soviet-made T-62 tank destroyed by the IDF and abandoned by the Syrians during the '73 War.

The old synagogue at Gamla, a ruined fortified town in the Golan. Gamla is aptly termed the "Masada of the North" because of the bloody battle fought here between Jewish rebels and three Roman legions under the command of (future) Emperor Vespasian. In the Jewish revolt of 66 AD 4,000 Jews were killed, and a further 5,000 were either murdered or jumped off the precipice to their death when Roman victory seemed imminent.

Banyas, from the greek Panaeas, was once the site of a
temple honoring this Greek god. With its springs and rivers,
the area is famous for its natural beauty and is a favorite
resort of the Israeli people.

A welder installs a parabolic solar collector.

# AN EXPRESSION OF SURVIVAL

"TECHNOLOGY IN ISRAEL IS SIMPLY AN EXpression of survival." It's a well-known statement that aptly characterizes the innovative and interrelated development of Israeli agriculture, military and industry since the earliest decades of Zionism. From the beginning pioneer days up to modern times, necessity has been the driving force behind innovation. Whether for crop irrigation or the latest improvement on a sophisticated weapons guidance system, necessity has taken on many guises: sometimes in the form of hostile neighbors or trade embargoes, at other times because of very limited natural resources.

Certainly it is historically evident that Jews throughout the ages have been developers and innovators, and as such accumulated tremendous knowledge in a wide variety of fields. But as Zionism became a political reality in the late 1800's, neccesity engendered a rethinking and reshaping of what had been traditional Jewish societies and roles. Trade, commerce, medicine, craftsmanship, rabbinical studies —these had been the primary professions of European Jews. Farming and soldiery were lacking, and these were *sine qua non* talents for creating a state.

Clearly many factors have contributed to the country's modern success: having the ability to draw upon skilled and educated people the world over from a multitude of professions; commitment to the Zionist dream; the need to produce products not available to the young nation due to distance from markets or world politics.

Former Member of Knesset, now industrialist, Stef Wertheimer has described the development of the Israeli economy as divided into three stages: First, meeting the agricultural subsistence requirements of the pioneer Zionists. Second, meeting the draining defense requirements of a community virtually under siege since the 1920s. Third, the development of a local high technology to the point where it's become a significant export industry. If one may trace threads, two are inseparable: expediency and academia.

From a reluctant importer of nearly all its basic necessities, Israel has developed into a leading exporter of agricultural produce and high-tech hardware. Uzia Galil, founder and CEO of Elron Electronic Industries, Ltd., sees that "the Israeli economy may be regarded as a pyramid supported by four legs: industry — in all its aspects, agriculture, academia and defense. It is the interplay of these four elements that accounts in large measure for the nation's real competitive advantage."

"At the beginning of the century," continues Galil, "the attitude was primarily how do you get settled on the land. For so many years the Jewish people have done everything else, but if you want to have a country, one of the first things you have to do is work the land. That first stage of Zionism was dedicated to settlement, land, and making a living through agriculture. Agriculture, with all the various forms of agriculture, the kibbutzim and everything, contributed to innovation, but innovation as such was strictly for very high class agriculture. At that time the concept of innovation and the engineering industry was very remote from the ideas of the country — for two reasons: one was that it would have interfered with pushing people to agriculture and settlement; the second, because we really didn't have any relative industrial advantage at that time," he observes.

In less than four decades Israel has made the transition from food dependency to food export. With the exception of cattle and grain, which are considered uneconomical to raise, Israel now produces 150% of its needs! Israel is not only a food export leader, but also a significant exporter of very advanced farm machinery systems. Drip irrigation — now almost a synonym for Israeli agricultural ingenuity — was introduced in the '60s by hydrologist Simha Blass, and it has been a success story ever since.

"The very basic problem that agriculture had in the beginning was the problem of different living standards in the pre-State times," observes Yoash Vaadia, agronomist and Vice President of Hebrew University.

"The Arab standard of living was mere subsistence because of the structure of their society; the Jewish standard of living was higher. The biggest problem was the competition and the cost of inputs between the Jewish and Arab societies.

"The Jews had expenses like big-time farmers but income like poor Arab *fellahin*. There was a problem of developing, planning, marketing and enhancing production system efficiency, because an economy which has its food produced with a donkey is very different from that which produces with a tractor and combine harvester. To fix a plan so that there would be an integrated economy was the biggest challenge," Vaadia remarks.

"The trick was to be able to pick up the old technologies that the Arabs were using, and work with those methods as we began a gradual transformation of improvement. I think what happened to Israeli agriculture was basically that. The first settlers used the local technology; they lived miserably, but they could fit themselves very easily into the existing system. They didn't bring technology from outside because they were not trained people. So there was this mixture of doing it the local way and improving on it because we had access to the rest of the world. Remember we came from Western civilization and we knew the ways Western civilization did things.

"Our system developed very quickly from old irrigation methods to what we got from California — a specific sprinkler system. Soon after that we moved to another, and then on to drip irrigation. So in my lifetime we have changed our citrus grove irrigation systems perhaps eight times."

"We had to go through a phase here when agriculture was not easy, with a lot of trials and errors," comments Amram Ashri, Professor at the Faculty of Agriculture at Hebrew University. "As we know, necessity is the mother of invention, but through this we accumulated a lot of knowledge and then developed our own research."

"This created a new concept in the strategy of the development of agriculture, all very much based on building upon existing technologies," remarks Alex Keynan, Professor of Microbiology and Parasitology at Hebrew University. "You see, the people who settled the country were not farmers in the traditional European sense. They were intellectuals who decided that farming is an ideology — back to the land, and back to physical work. They looked at their Jewish *luftenproletariat* which was always floating on society and never really earned an honest day of work. That was where their ideas arose to start a new ideology.

"Now those people usually had a good background, and they were willing to experiment — especially in the Kibbutz Movement, where they were more able to take risks. You know in a single farm, a man who takes many risks loses everything. The Kibbutz Movement took about 10% of its resources in risks. And if it failed, so what? Especially if they had national support. So you had a farming population which was very willing to experiment. Thus Israel was perhaps the first country in this part of the world to develop a real science-based agriculture."

Expanding on that, Amram Ashri observes that, "the agricultural achievements are a very fine combination of research, farmers, and extension programs. There is a very close and sometimes very informal cooperation, because for one thing, about ⅓ of our students are either from the moshavim or the kibbutzim, and many of them go back to the farms to actually farm. Look, it's very easy. If my colleague here works in cotton, and if he wants to try a new procedure, he can call on ten of his ex-students from different parts of the country and ask if they would be willing to put in a few rows of his new breeding line. And they do it.

"Another way is that they bring the problems to our attention, informally, not through channels. He says, 'I've got a problem — what can you offer?' Sometimes these things lead to some very interesting innovations."

Desert makes up 65% of Israel, but it's not considered a wasteland but a challenge. Ben-Gurion's memoirs *Recollections* include many observations on the Negev: "The capacity for creativity and pioneering strength of Israel will be tested, and this test will be crucial. In the Negev scientific aptitude and Jewish research will be tested...to concentrate on fields of research for which northern nations didn't have need."

The Jacob Blaustein Institute for Desert Research at Sde Boker is an extension of Ben-Gurion University of the Negev. It focuses on research and development of arid zones; in particular, the conversion of the Negev into a productive environment. It's a true marriage of science, agriculture and environment, with innovative satellite projects in solar energy, desert architecture, hydrology and meteorology, hydrobiology and geo-botany, ecology, social sciences and others.

Professor Amos Richmond, the Institute's first Chairman, describes one of his intriguing projects. "One could think much about the ocean water that laces the deserts the world over; so we learn how to work with saline water. One solution, not the only solution mind you, is to grow algae. These are water plants indeed, but they are saline water plants. They can serve various purposes: for food and feed — they are rich in protein. Also for pigments and all kinds of chemicals. As a matter of fact, except for wood and fibers, algae can be used for almost anything that people can extract from the organic world.

"This is agricultural microbiology: a new field, unsterile microbiology. For some people it's crazy, it's difficult, but it can be done. The question is can we grow it economically? There is a very high potential and there is a lot yet to be learned, but I am certain this will be an important innovation the world over in the next century."

**B**rainpower — Israel's only real natural resource, has been nurtured in the academic institutions long before the founding of the State. Development of higher education institutes such as Hebrew University, the Technion and the Weizmann Institute was of paramount importance for the very existence and future prosperity of the nation.

"I would say that one of our greatest achievements is the creation of a high-level academic community,"

notes Professor Alex Keynan. "The pre-State years are rather interesting...one should remember that science preceded the State of Israel by something like 30 years. Science then was a purely pragmatic process, first created to serve the needs of the very small Jewish population here in Palestine.

"In order to understand Israeli science and education, you have to understand its roots back at the beginning of the century. At the time there was a split in the Zionist outlook. The Zionist objective was the establishment of a Jewish state; the nature of that state was not much discussed. The only agreement was that it was to be sovereign.

"The first group was headed by Ahad Ha'am, the philosopher. He said, 'Look, we don't want to solve the problems of the Jews. We want to solve the problem of Judaic culture. It has lost its center.' So people like Magnes, Buber, and Ahad Ha'am thought Jerusalem should be a spiritual center instead of the State of Israel. This was the idea behind Hebrew University. In a sense it was not to be a teaching university, but a spiritual center for Jews from all over.

"But there were other people of the Jewish intellectual elite who were less extreme. They said let's integrate Zionist ideals with other things which are more pragmatic. The first and greatest of these was [Chaim] Weizmann. He was a main-line Zionist, and all his life he did everything to achieve that state. But he never did anything to diminish the spiritual dimension of it. He was a middle-man between factions. Magnes, Buber and Ahad Ha'am didn't care about Zionism. What they really wanted was a very strong spiritual center.

"Remember that the Zionist movement was basically anti-religious; they had no intentions of waiting for the Messiah. I remember my father when we came to Warsaw, *schlepping* me to the different Jewish religious quarters, 'See these people?' he said. 'They're silly. They're stupid waiting for the Messiah. We're not going to do this,' " Keynan recalls across a fifty-year gap. "My father was a member of the First Zionist Congress. He was very busy in the movement. He spent half the year in Europe and half the year in Palestine from 1922 on. So when he spoke about a 'spiritual' center, he really meant an intellectual center.

"Now how do you translate an intellectual center into anything concrete like a university?" asks Keynan rhetorically. "We had a group of people like Einstein and Paul Erlich — the Nobel prize winner who developed the first drug against syphilis. Most of the important early people came out for ideological reasons and really wanted to start something here. And it also created a strong link with the world intellectual community. The whole Jewish elite all over the world rallied behind the idea of having a spiritual center that was really an intellectual center.

"And they got the ear of the Rothschilds, both British and French branches of that family, and they had the Warburgs on their committee, so they had access to money. Ben-Gurion himself was one of the people who adopted the philosophy of wanting to have a sovereign state, but he also wanted this state to have a spiritual dimension. He didn't want a bi-national state, but he did want a spiritual element.

"Ben-Gurion was a very strong believer in science, and supported it very strongly. And I must say that it was the Mapai government that quickly went in the direction of trying to support universities, to establish science. From this point up to '73 we always had strong support from government. '73 was a watershed. From that time onwards so much of the national resources went into defense, that the treasury had to cut in all kinds of places. Cuts began in higher education without enough sources of alternative revenue. It was very difficult because education in this country was always built on a system which supported not only teaching but had a combinant of research in it."

The Weizmann Institute in Rehovot was founded in the '30s with funding from the Seiff family, proprietors of a large chain of English department stores. Professor William Taub recalls the early days. "There were only 12 scientists at that time and we studied whatever we chose. Mostly it was pure science, as well as projects connected with Israel's economy: citrus, dairy, silk,

tobacco and pharmaceuticals. When the war broke out we were needed by the State to produce things we couldn't get from abroad — particularly drugs for the Allied forces in the Middle East. We did a lot of work with malaria remedies, continuing up until the '50s.

"Now in the '50s there was a new breed of scientist: nuclear engineers. So then we worked on pure scientific research: organic and inorganic chemistry, bacteriology, virology, polymer research, isotope research and so on. In the '60s another new group of scientists came in, and again the focus changed. We did more applied research, as the majority of the researchers felt it was important to produce things needed by humanity. Now we do much more applied research, but on the side we do our pure research.

"That scientists can do whatever kinds of research they like is one of the nicest things about being part of the Institute. There is a real feeling of trust that you are doing your job."

For several decades there was heated debate over the immediate requirements of the Yishuv taking precedence over pure science. "Those scientists who came here from Europe suddenly found themselves in a funny situation. They came here to establish a spiritual center, but they suddenly found themselves in an unknown, hostile environment," comments Professor Keynan. "Agriculture was primitive; they couldn't grow anything. Nobody knew anything about the country's natural resources. There was no geological or hydrological mapping. So our very first objective was to understand our environment.

"We now had these scholars who had to deal with immediate applied science needs, and we got this special mixture — perhaps more typical of Israeli science than elsewhere — of some very good basic scientists now beginning to solve applied problems," Keynan recalls. "To give you an example of applied problems, whole parts of the country couldn't be settled because of malaria. So a group of research microbiologists and parasitologists, under Professor Kliegler, created a field station in the Galil. Professor Goldblum became head of the station, and by the mid '30s they had completely eradicated malaria.

"This is the way our basic research group started to deal with applied problems. If you go to any scientific community here in Israel, you'll find that many of them have gone in two directions. You don't see this very much in the United States, where evolutions in technology are picked up by industry two days later.

"Up until the '70s," continues Keynan, "there was a very strong university emphasis on basic research. I was Chairman of the National Research Council until 1968. Our committee looked at the structure of Israeli science and decided that while we had a strong component of basic research, and good applied research in agriculture and medicine, there was very little research in industrial fields. The government then decided to give its chief scientists means to develop applied research. There was funding for this from outside sources; for example, the Ministry of Agriculture would give money to the University. As long as the University had some sort of free operational money, it could fund most of its basic research. But as the University budget shrank, it became more and more dependent on outside funds, so more and more outside budgets were created for industrial and applied research outside the University."

"By 1980 you had a complete reversal of the pyramid. Now a large part of national resources go into applied research, much of it outside the universities. Even a lot of university research is financed from applied sources, resulting in the basic research potential of the country going down. Now our National Academy is trying to establish something similar to your National Science Foundation, because there is a real danger to the basic research future of the country. It will take big efforts to reconstruct it in some way," concludes Keynan with a warning.

Since his days as Defense Minister in Yitzhak Rabin's government, Shimon Peres has been a major advocate for developing high tech independence and moving toward high tech export by Israeli business. He has written that "the Technion today is the most important

resource we have to train the vital manpower needed in order to realize Israel's central goal: to transform our country into one whose economy is based on science and technology."

Uzia Galil, Chairman of the Board of Governors at the Technion for the last 8 years, agrees and understands the benefits implicit in the marriage of industry and the higher learning institutes. "I consider education very, very important, and that's why I am giving considerable time to the Technion. After all, they have provided 70% of the engineers in this country. You can also see some other interesting pictures. The aeronautical faculty at the Technion was developed much *before* there was an aircraft industry. That means there was a certain vision that if at a future point in time you will want an aircraft industry, then you had better start to build the knowledge base.

"But there was a big risk. In 1952-3, when that faculty started, the objective of the aircraft industry was only to repair planes and nothing else. Without the vision of the Faculty of Aeronautics at the Technion to build this industry, the Kfir or the Lavi, or everything else could never have been possible."

Certainly Galil speaks with authority. As founder and CEO of Elron Electronics Industries, Ltd., Uzia Galil has developed some of Israel's most successful and innovative high-tech companies, many from academic concepts. "Our whole concept at Elron is to identify small entrepreneurial teams. When we conclude they have good technology and a good product in mind, and the market is there, we initially nurse them as part of Elron. They grow, and after they reach a certain level, we provide the financing and marketing support. They know that if they are successful they will be spun off into an independent, and finally public company. This way they can really make money, because they will work on their own stuff. It's a combination of what you would call venture capital, plus the large corporation nursing approach. We try to give our people the best of both worlds."

Eli Hurvitz, CEO and Managing Director of Teva Pharmaceuticals, expounds on a similar approach. "In our research and development activities, we do a lot with the Weizmann Institute, other higher learning institutions, and university hospitals. In our R&D and search for new molecules and new products, we have approximately four new products in the pipeline. Only one is our idea; three of them were invented by people from the research institutes. To be more precise, the ideas were developed and, in a sense, proven there. We take and change them from an idea into a pharmaceutical product. As you know, the higher learning and research institutions here are exceptionally good. In the past we used to wait until they came to us with an idea; now we can go to them. We have funds we have developed with a few of the institutions for the researchers in specific fields of pharmaceuticals. If we are interested in an idea, we finance it from the very beginning and the results are quite interesting."

Nowhere else in Israel is necessity more the mother of invention than in the military. The struggle to survive against bigger and better-armed implacable enemies has created a disproportionally large military establishment. Despite a great drain of resources, this military build-up produced technology which has spurred not only industry and widely divergent high-tech endeavors, but interdisciplinary cooperation as well.

"After the creation of the State, agriculture, settlement, and innovation continued, but additionally there came a major effort in defense: and defense brought in technology," recalls Uzia Galil. "So you had agriculture, you had defense, and you had some kind of local industry that really was not so innovative because the whole idea was to create jobs. At the time there was one consideration: jobs. No matter how much it costs; it's efficient, it's not efficient — just create jobs. The only innovations at that time were related to agriculture or to defense. It was only later on, at the end of the '60s, that one started to see industrial innovation not directly related to defense or agriculture."

"The basis of Israeli military technology goes back to well before the War of 1948, back to the days of the Palmach. People then began to grasp the fact that Israel was much smaller and weaker than the countries it would soon be fighting," outlines Hebrew University Professor Gerald Steinberg, an academic analyst of military affairs. "So one of the best ways to make up for that tremendous gap was through applied technology. Thus the Science Corps was founded in '48, although there were few resources or monies. It was not designed to build up an academic infrastructure with the Universities, but designed to solve problems and remedy shortages in the desperately short time period the military was faced with.

"There was no artillery, so the Science Corps devised some backyard things. They took tubes stuffed with homemade explosives with which they could pound away at short range. In the '40s and '50s, a lot of Israeli arms were second or third hand; there was even stuff from World War I! Many of these weapons were missing parts and had no replacements, so you had to come up with some sort of makeshift system," he explains.

"After the '56 and '67 wars, Israel captured large quantities of Soviet-made armor and artillery for which they now had to manufacture ammunition. They even sold their surplus production to other countries, and did improvement work on *Soviet* tanks. IMI [Israeli Military Industries] openly advertised their services on a commercial basis. We'll take your Russian tanks and refit and recondition them for you!"

"In the early '50s," remembers Professor Keynan, "the situation was such that we had so much money for military weapons that the generals and the Chief of Staff said 'Let's buy weapons.' So they had a choice: buy weapons or start a military development which would take ten years to evolve something. It was the wisdom of Ben-Gurion, and to a great extent of Shimon Peres that the whole military research establishment was created. And of course this movement received a 'blessing' from DeGaulle when he declared a moratorium on arms supplies to Israel in '67."

When Uzia Galil served in the navy he was in charge of electronics research and development. "The defense establishment was the first one in Israel to understand the importance of spending a lot of money in R&D. In the '50s, before anyone in this country thought about putting a penny into our research and development, you found that the military establishment was already investing R&D money in technology.

"When we set up Elbit, it was with know-how from the Ministry of Defense. Now the real step happened in '66-7, because there was a very close tie between Israel and France. By that time Israel had contributed a lot to the development of the French aviation industry, and when that link got cut off, there was a major decision: to invest in R&D."

"And that is exactly what happened," explains Gerald Steinberg "There was a tremendous emphasis on using the available technical infrastructure to overcome the quantitative gap with Israel's Arab enemies. In general, the Israeli ability to adapt older technology is better than the Arabs' ability to employ newer technology. There's a great emphasis in the Israeli educational system on the adaptation of technology, whereas in the Arab states there's a great deal of illiteracy. Therefore there's a great deal of trouble in maintaining sophisticated equipment. So as the Arabs increase their quantitative advantage, the Israelis increase their qualitative advantage. Very roughly, one may say that the military balance is maintained in that way.

"The first real use of modern Israeli technology came in the '67 War. The Israeli air force, for example, was the first air force in the world to have an all-jet force. It was a small air force, so it didn't take that much, but in the early '60s the decision was made to go for a smaller number of high-quality aircraft. In '67 this decision proved itself, illustrating how Israel is always two or three steps ahead in the use of technology.

"If you go back to '48," Steinberg continues, "Israeli military technology was done in the most pragmatic of ways. I'll give you a recent example where the same philosophy holds, and that was the development of the RPV, or the remote pilotless vehicle called the 'Mastiff.' It was developed because of a specific need to gather real-time intelligence pictures over the battlefield. But the Israelis just couldn't go in and buy it anywhere. The Americans were working on some super-sophisticated,

multi-million dollar project called the 'Aquila', but you can't buy one because it doesn't work yet. So the Israelis defined a clear requirement and told themselves they had a couple of years to build such a thing. They did, for even less than a tenth of what the Americans have put into their project. It's a much simpler system, but you can put up ten for the price of one American RPV.

"The Lavi project, a locally-built multi-purpose fighter bomber, has been a major watershed for the Israeli defense industry. Instead of Israel becoming a major weapons exporter, the decision not to build the Lavi caused us to realize we ought to put more of our money and resources into civil technology and its spin-offs and less into the military. There was tremendous national debate over it for about a year, but finally it was decided by the Cabinet — in a very close vote — that it would come out so much more expensive than originally expected that the project should be shelved for now. It would have cost the equivalent of at least one year's GNP!

"First of all, since we're realistically not going to be able to compete with the Americans, the French, the Russians — even the Chinese — let's focus more on our immediate needs. But there are certain things we can do to limit the amount of foreign dependence; we have ways of filling gaps, of adapting weapons made for the central European front for the Israeli theater.

"Militarily we worry about the capability of the other sides," Steinberg explains. "For now only Syria seems to have the military strength to threaten Israel. But Israelis worry, and there's good historical reason, especially when you look back to '48 or '73. In a very short period of time the regional balance of power could turn around. It's the job of the Israeli military to worry about what happens if Iran and Iraq make peace tomorrow, and then Iraq turns around and starts marching into Jordan. But if the Iraqis, like in '48 and '67, would march right through Jordan, we have to worry that the Iraqis could be right there with the Syrians even though right now they're at each other's throats.

"The capability of the Iraqis, combined with the Syrians, is serious. The Egyptians could turn around also. With inter-Arab politics, that situation could change in a short time. Still, the Egyptian peace agreement made a very big difference," declares Steinberg. "We have to worry, but we don't have to worry about today or tomorrow. It means that a lot of the resources that went into defense against Egypt are now free for use elsewhere."

Even though a disproportionate amount of Israel's GNP must be devoted to the military, there certainly have been positive offshoots for society. Uzia Galil feels that educated people are a primary benefit to the civilian sector. "A lot of the people who left the military and set up new things in commercial industries, basically had the benefit of that education. Some of the first computer guys came from that area, as well as managers, electronics engineers, and much of the technical infrastructure.

"In order to produce a CT scanner for medical imaging, for instance, you need the know-how and mechanical infrastructure that was built by the military. Many people think that you can take the same military industry and just put out commercial products, that doesn't work, at least I don't believe it. I believe that the defense industry creates an infrastructure of subcontractors and support industries," observes Galil.

Israel's export economy is increasingly based on high-tech products developed from local innovation and scientific know-how. Nearly one-third of total export income is derived from this industry, and that proportion is expected to increase. "Today, specialized, high-technology industry has taken center stage," Yigal Erlich, Chief Scientist of Israel's Ministry of Industry has stated. "Israel's economic development depends on expanding its industrial exports, and these exports are increasingly high-tech oriented."

"Let's start with what we want in this country," suggests Uzia Galil. "If one assumes that we want to see a country that is very attractive to the young generation that was born here, and attractive to the young generation from abroad that may want to come and live here, then it's obvious that we want a very prosperous society with challenges and a high quality of life. Now in every society you look and see what your relative advantages are, what you have and what you have not. It's very easy to say what we have not. We certainly don't have a lot of men and we certainly do not have very many natural resources except, to a limited extent, some of the Dead Sea. But one of the few things that we do have are people that are intrigued by new developments. On the average they have a learning capability as good as anyone in the Western World to use that knowledge to a society's financial benefit. I think we are lucky that the world is continually changing in the last decades in the direction that more and more of the economy is really dependent on the intelligent use of knowledge," Galil notes.

"Therefore, that opens the possibility to create the kind of an industry that does not require many natural resources, the heavy machinery or the extreme capital investments for fixed assets where again we don't have very many advantages. In order for any society to have the right standard of life, it has to be economically independent which we are not. In order to become financially independent you either just have enough population to create everything to live by yourself, or you have somehow to export more than you import. So you arrive at the conclusion that exports are the key to economic independence."

Technology can build the better mousetrap, but successful distribution is key to capitalizing on such an innovation. Israel is at a geographical disadvantage; the natural markets are the Arabs, but the political ambiance is decidedly hostile. Realizing the economic benefit vital for prosperity and security will neccesitate a combination of old fashioned *chutzpah*, funding, and the ability to find and anticipate new markets.

"I strongly believe that the future of building high technology lies in companies with one leg in Israel and one in the US with connections in Europe as well," opines Galil. "This configuration is necessary to enhance exports and market access. I think you will find that on a comparative scale entrepreneurial business in Israel has developed very much similar to the way it developed in the US. We will get in business all over the world because we believe that a small country has to operate globally but there must be some added value. What we are looking for is increased added value for export because the only kinds of things we sell locally are for defense. Everything else is primarily export, and we are looking only at business that has a major potential for growth."

Chief Financial Officer Dan Suesskind of Teva Pharmaceuticals claims, "it is, of course, not worthwhile to develop a product just for the Israeli market, so if you want to go into more sophisticated products and develop something new, you first have to look for outside markets. Usually when Israelis are going to the US they see a David and Goliath: little David is going to the huge American market to compete."

"Although I remember who won the fight between David and Goliath, we found that after we analyzed the American market that we are not going to fight the Goliaths," concedes Eli Hurvitz. "Because we are not going to compete with Merck and Cyanamid and Squibb and others, we have started our American operation together with a *small* American company, W.R. Grace," he laughs. "And we are going to compete with generic companies; in size most of them are smaller than we are, but in sophistication many are a few steps lower. For the American market we intend to go with only those products where we have a relative advantage either by know-how or by efficiency."

"New markets are very tough," Uzia Galil admits. "The entrance fee becomes much greater, but obviously there is potential. The basic rule for the Israeli high tech manager is to see how to take an existing technology in some existing market and add something to make it better. If you look at Optrotech's vision systems for the inspection of the circuit boards, they were the first that came on the market with a computerized system. That's an application of artificial intelligence to replace the human inspection of circuit boards with magnifying glasses and so on, with a computer electro-optical controlled system. It's an existing technology. The sensors exist, the computers exist, the software exists, but it's the application of existing technology to a new market.

"Now let's remember the defense market; that's a very major part of the export industry in this country. If you take a company like Elbit that was originally selling more in Israel, today we have 60% exports. What is their relative advantage? Again, it is employing existing technology, and putting it together with a user in a cost-effective way. That's where you can penetrate.

"Israel is the highest exporter in the world in terms of GNP. We export about 50% of our GNP, and you won't find this in any other country. In Japan — everybody is speaking about Japan — it's less than 20%. In the States, it is less than 10%. Usually you find that small countries trade much more than big countries, relative to their GNP. They have no alternative; they can't produce everything in such a small market. I hope that one of these days, when there is peace in the Middle East, that we could access local markets."

Technological exports may be on the rise, but agriculture has always been the mainstay of the export economy. In less than four decades Israel's agriculture has become a major export industry. Amram Ashri has been instrumental in the development of agriculture to meet export potential. "Today, after a period of rapid innovation, we are at a bit of a crossroads. You see, when the State of Israel was established, in the mid-1940s and through the '50s, we had a shortage of food. There weren't enough eggs, not enough milk, not enough meat. So our first priority was to produce enough food. In the '60s we reached the stage where we supplied our needs and then started exporting the surpluses. It wasn't yet production for export; we were exporting the extra amount, which is not exactly the right way.

"Then Minister of Agriculture Dayan, General Moshe Dayan, made a very big push for export-oriented agriculture: the greenhouses, cut flowers, fruit, all kinds of things of that type. If Europe eats avocados today, it is because of Israeli doing."

"It doesn't pay us to supply all our needs in everything," notes Professor Ashri. "For instance, it pays us to produce roasting peanuts for consumers and sell them on the international market. Then we turn around and buy soybeans to make oil rather than growing peanuts for oil. It's pure economics. We know to produce the things that are to our advantage."

"Israel plans to continue expanding her imports," states Professor Vaadia. "The whole idea of exports in Israel is based on the simple observation that we are land and water poor. These are two major things that one needs for food production. But we have sophisticated agricultural technology, so the whole philosophy of Israeli agriculture differs in principle from that, say, of Canada or America where originally agriculture wasn't designed for export. In Israel we philosophically don't work to provide food for the population. We think it's cheaper to bring wheat from Kansas. There is hardly any wheat here today because there is no way to economically compete with Kansas growers," explains Vaadia.

"So what we do is take our expensive water and export it. Then we import cheap water — that's our philosophy. We bring in wheat from Kansas and soya beans from Iowa; they provide food for our people. We then use our expensive water for exporting flowers, avocados, mangoes and citrus. So the idea is that our exports should provide the cost for the import of the rest of the food. If we look at agriculture, we try to be independent; the economics of it sometimes are and sometimes are not."

"We have to find our niche in the market," Amram Ashri explains. "If we are to compete on the higher quality levels, then we need a higher level of organization. We are aiming at more sophisticated products; for instance we send to South America four hundred banana plants in a box just larger than a cigarette pack. They are reproduced through tissue culture, allowing us to reproduce and clean them from viruses by making the cells reproduce faster than the virus.

"There are many things we can do for export. We can produce seeds, we can innovate and come up with new varieties all the time, keep these for ourselves for several years, and always have something new. This takes long term research, a lot of coordination, and patience — you don't want to make mistakes."

Certainly Israel is in a unique position; in many respects it's as developed as any First World country, yet it still reflects Third World characteristics. Politically there is isolation, but the sharing of knowledge is an Israeli trait, and one that should certainly help transcend political/religious differences.

"Israel is a very small country, but it is at a unique crossroads in terms of technology, geography and motivation," says Amram Ashri. "We have the conditions of many developing countries, and we have the science and technology of the developed countries — we speak both languages. We are not smarter than the English, or the French or the Americans; but I grew up on a small farm and still plowed with a horse and milked the family cows and goats by hand. You don't have that generation of farmers left in the States anymore. They may be experts in dairy, but they know only the complicated, computer-operated machine. You can't do that in Senegal or in Guam. Don't forget that many of the people that came to Israel as immigrants in the '50s didn't know anything about modern agriculture. We settled them on the land and trained them, so we have this experience as well.

"Because agriculture is one of the most creative facets of Israel, people in many countries know us and they look to us for cooperation, assistance and the like. Many years ago, in the beginning, the big effort came when Golda Meir was Foreign Minister. She gave a big push to Israel's scientific, agricultural and medical cooperation with developing countries."

The spread of knowledge has always been vital for Israeli scientists; some even harbor a quasi-Biblical Messianism for it. "All Israelis know a little bit of the Bible. It is written that from Zion we will spread the Torah (the knowledge), and I believe that the knowledge that we really can spread is desert science," notes Moshe Shackak, an ecologist at the Institute for

Desert Research, "All the concepts of the desert are important to Israel, but most important is to transfer that knowledge to other places. If you accept that ⅔ of Israel is desert, one thing that Israel can work together with other people on is desert. People even think that we know more about the desert then we really do. Two years ago a colleague of mine from Pakistan said 'You Jewish people, you know so much about the desert.' 'No,' I said, 'we really don't.' He said, 'Oh, you just don't want to tell me all your secrets!' But I had told him the truth. I have been studying the desert for 20 years, and everyday I know less."

Professor Amos Richmond of the Institute continues his colleague's thoughts, "People are trying to get technology to Third World countries, and surely the scientific community has something to give to other people. We are a lot more liberal, and realize that we have to develop peaceful relations. We have to step into the other side's shoes and view the problems. The academic community in Israel realizes this, and has found that when we go abroad we associate with 'the enemy' and they associate with us. Many times it's not easy, because once everybody returns back to his country, those lines of communication are forbidden. With time this will change, but I don't know how."

If political change comes only with difficulty to the Middle East, at least Moshe Shackak may have a way of encouraging it. "Instead of *throwing* stones, we have found a way to collect them in order to catch water and use it to increase production of the desert environment. We who have been born in Israel know that the Arabs and Bedouins are part of this land. The problem is not that they will push us or we will push them, the problem is how to live together — and the desert is a good place to start. Besides, here tension is not so high as in Judea and Samaria. Now we use their [Bedouin] culture and combine it with our scientific knowledge to create the first Bedouin scientific station in the world. They will be a part of it, not just we Jewish people teaching them what to do.

"We found a way to plant trees in an area that has just 90mm of rainfall — and not plant them in the valleys. We found out that you can plant on the slope, which is considered a place that trees are not able to grow. They came to us and said, 'trees in this place? It's a miracle!' Of course we can explain why, so that's exactly what we are doing. The knowledge was where to dig the catchments, and the trees are planted without any additional water after planting. 'Let nature work by itself,' we said, and found a way to increase the production of the desert that will help many countries in the Third World. We would like to solve the problems of human relations and production together.

"On the West Bank it is different. You can see that the Arabs have cultivated most of the land. The destruction to the land there is because so many wars have been waged over that territory, that small piece of land. In spite of the fact that politically we are in quite a confrontation with them, agriculturally our cooperation is quite good.

"So all of the relations with Jews and Arabs are multidimensional. What you read in the newspaper is one dimensional. It may be the truth, but the truth is complex and it depends on what hierarchical levels you are dealing. Even if it seems like a paradox, there are hierarchy levels on which we are in a very friendly and cooperative relationship with the Arabs. On other levels we are ready to kill each other. I am not a politician, I'm a scientist, but I believe this is the only way."

"With Jordan we have a lot of activity that has taken many forms after the Six Day War when we took over the West Bank," notes Professor Amram Ashri as he discusses work being done by the Hebrew University Faculty of Agriculture. "There was an agricultural extension service there with farm advisors for Judea. We left it all there and just brought in an infusion of a few very good Israeli experts. The story of the agricultural development in the West Bank is a beautiful case history. For agricultural development you need knowhow, capital, markets, and you need people who will be willing to learn. All these things combined very well there. Now vegetables and fruit from the West Bank and the Gaza Strip go all the way to Iraq and Saudi Arabia. That cooperation was started by Mr. Gojani, head of the Farm Advisory Extension Service in the West Bank in Judea.

"Every week, on Friday, he would go to Amman. You know the distance from Jerusalem to Amman? 45 miles or one hour, but it takes some time for formalities on both sides. Every Friday he would go to the Ministry in Amman and pass on the know-how. We would no sooner innovate something on this side of the Jordan than it could be seen on the other side. We no sooner introduce a new variety of cucumber, and the seeds make their way to the other side.

"By the way we do sell seeds and various other agricultural products to other countries, sometimes through intermediaries. Much of the cooperation is done bilaterally through the US. I cooperate with you and Mr. Muhammad cooperates with you but really we are unofficially cooperating with each other.

"Cooperation with Egypt is also a very interesting thing. You know we have been meeting with scientists from Egypt for many years, and when we met them unofficially communications were good, but it could not go beyond. I remember the first delegation of researchers who came here after the peace treaty was signed. Initially there was a bit of strangeness, but after the first five minutes we realized that our problems were the same. In agriculture, even if you don't know the language you can communicate with another man. You hold the soil or the plant in your hands; you show him, and he understands.

"Agricultural cooperation with Egypt is continuing and growing all the time. Even during times of official coolness we still cooperate — they still have to feed their people. We sometimes say that if we want to strengthen agricultural relations we should break diplomatic relations!"

The fight for survival over insurmountable odds has its rewards. Professor Vaadia expands, "I think what typifies Israel's success is considerable education for joint national success. I'm not aware of many other societies that have had that much education and that much mutual responsibility between its people. What typifies Israeli society is the feeling of a family, a feeling of belonging. The success of Labor Zionism was what led that spirit."

Eli Hurvitz agrees. "One of the beautiful things about this country that we Israelis enjoy is the fact that you are important here. If you manage a company in the States even 50 times the size, who cares? But here they do, and if one exports over $1 million he is invited by the president of the State to his house. It's not only that you are invited, that is just a symbol, it's that you have really contributed something to the country."

"In a way," comments Amram Ashri, "the contribution of the individual in Israel can be much more significant than in a place like the United States. Simply take my case, I had many offers to stay in the US to work for the USDA Research Service, interesting work, too. But first I had my roots here — parents, commitment, idealism, Zionism — call it what you want. Secondly, there is only one college of agriculture here in Israel — it's this one, and I am the one that brought the teaching of genetics and breeding to this faculty. If I do a good job, the future agronomists of Israel will have good knowledge; if I do a bum job, there is no Purdue, Cornell, UCLA, University of Illinois, or Minnesota and so on to fill the gap. So the contribution of the individual can be much more meaningful and much more significant."

Despite all the achievements, Israel's struggles are far from over. There must be new and continual goals to attain if the country is to survive. Uzia Galil cautions, "If we are not careful, we could easily become an exporter of people and not products and technology. If we do not act wisely today, there will be no economic infrastructure for the new immigrants that we seek to entice to Israel. And there will be few incentives for our own young people to remain in an economic climate that would become stagnant. The trick is to keep advancing and learning. We can no longer be so reliant on either world Jewry or our strategic importance to the West. We simply cannot procrastinate any longer. Either we accept tomorrow's challenges or we jeopardize and mortgage our future." ■

FAR LEFT: Green house "tunnels" of sheet plastic protect new plants from the elements, retard evaporation, lengthen growing season.
LEFT: Golden wheat from the Galilee.
BELOW: Here in the Jezre'el Valley, as elsewhere in Israel, flowers grown for export have become an important crop.
Since the founding of the State, Israeli agriculture has progressed from bare subsistence to a profitable export industry.

FAR LEFT: Odet Denebom forcefeeds his geese at Moshav Tel Adiqim in the Jezre'el Valley. Israel is one of the world's leading producers of foie gras.
ABOVE: Momo Levinowitz sprays a field at Moshav Neot Hakkiker. Moshavs produce most of the crops marketed on the local level.
LEFT: Melon harvest at Neot Hakkiker, near the Dead Sea. Having attained virtual self-sufficiency, Israeli agronomists are now able to produce crops solely for export, sustaining an important source of foreign exchange.

ABOVE: Fish breeding ponds in the Hula Valley. Fish is becoming an important export commodity.
RIGHT: Goldfish at the Institute for Desert Research at Sde Boker. One of the many goals of the Institute is the development of science-based rather than resource-based agriculture for arid lands. This project is researching commercially viable species, including goldfish, eel and catfish, which can be raised in the brackish water abundant in the Negev Desert aquifers.
FAR RIGHT: Algae aeration tanks at the Microalgal Laboratory. The premise is that microalgae can be raised as an economical, renewable source for food, feed, raw materials and energy; a resource which can be produced advantageously in warm arid areas employing brackish or sea water. Currently such projects are funded by commercially-interested groups, including Kibbutz Industries.

*BELOW: Irrigation in the arid Jordan Valley.*
*OPPOSITE: A kibbutznik from Nof Ginnosar works with hybrid banana plants. Seedlings of this variety are exported to South America; crops flourishing due to efficient irrigation in the Sharon Plain; banana manager at Kibbutz Nasholim at the valve controls of his intricate watering system; citrus trees in the Negev Desert growing with drip irrigation piping. Efficient and sophisticated irrigation is imperative in this nation of very limited water resources, and a variety of methods are employed according to specific requirements.*
*Although Israel's agricultural output has increased dramatically over recent decades, water consumption has remained at virtually the same level. One of the most efficient systems is drip irrigation, invented by Israeli agronomist Simcha Blass. Nothing is wasted on open ground; only the individual plants receive their measured amount of water, fertilizer and pesticides through the central system.*

154

*TOP: The desert can become habitable, fertile land if brought to life with judicious use of water.*
*ABOVE, LEFT: Rows of citrus trees at Kibbutz Sde Boker, and cabbages at Nishor Zahad in the Arava Valley are examples of some of the agricultural feats performed in the desert.*
*OPPOSITE: Kibbutz Sde Boker was founded in 1952 by former soldiers in the Negev, whose goal was to make the desert bloom. After decades of government service, former Prime Minister David Ben-Gurion chose to retire here.*

*Some time-tested agricultural endeavors remain unchanged by the progress of modern technology.*
*RIGHT: A Bedouin girl herds her goats on scrubland along the Beersheba-Dimona road. Goats do well because they can exist on marginal land.*
*BELOW: An Arab farmer laborously ploughing his field by horse.*
*OPPOSITE: A fisherman from Old Jaffa prepares sardine bait for his night's fishing. The traditional lanterns attract the fish to the bait; another fisherman in the soft light of dusk casts his net into the Mediterranean Sea.*

Examples of Israel's
modern architecture.
ABOVE: The IBM
building, Tel Aviv.
LEFT: Dan Hotel, Tel Aviv.
OPPOSITE: The Etzion
Block Yeshiva in Allon
Shevut, Judea.

*A trompe d'oeil wall painting, Tel Aviv.*

OPPOSITE: An aerial photo of new housing developments in Ramot (Jerusalem); soldiers walk through an underground in Tel Aviv; Ramot's unusual prismic modular houses: even the inside walls slope! A mud brick house in a UNWRA refugee camp near Jericho.
BELOW: A new, stabilized adobe house at the Desert Research Institute. Adobe is inexpensive and thermally more efficient than concrete, therefore it is ideal for desert housing. Unfortunately there is a great deal of resistance to the use of adobe in contemporary construction due to psychological associations that equate mud houses with refugee camps.

*Traditional industry: A coastal electric generating plant near Hadera. Purchased from the United States, it still uses fossil fuels, the old standby.*

ABOVE: A Dead Sea Works plant near Dimona, where potash
and bromine are processed. The mineral resources of the
Dead Sea have been successfully exploited for decades.
RIGHT: A minerals conveyor system near Hadera.
OPPOSITE: Dry bulk storage hoppers in the northern Galilee.

*RIGHT: Electronic intelligence post on the Syrian border. BELOW: Tactical display on board Israeli submarine. Local electronics firms such as Elbit have gained world-wide repute for their quality guidance systems.*

LEFT: Helicopter lands
on Israeli navy Sa'ar
missile boat.
BELOW: Interior of a
mobile army tactical
command center.

RIGHT: Cockpit of a Kfir fighter-bomber showing Elbit weapons delivery and navigation systems.
BELOW: Completing one of the three prototypes of the Lavi fighter-bomber. Following stormy debate the government decided to purchase US-made F-16s instead of risking the enormous investment required to develop its own aircraft.

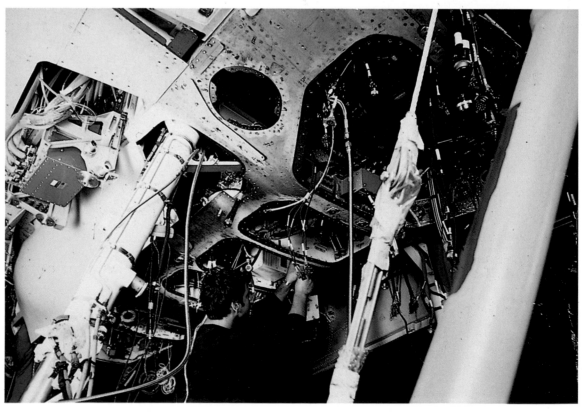

ABOVE: Wind tunnel testing the Kfir fighter-bomber at the Haifa Technion. The successful Kfir is an Israeli-built hybrid: a French Mirage airframe built under license powered by a US-made General Electric J-79 engine.

LEFT: Automation in armaments production: MIG welding armor plating on the hull of a "Merkava" tank. Now in its third production version, the Merkava has proven to be a highly successful main battle tank. Never again in times of trouble will Israel have to go begging on the world market for a tank weapons platform.

*The 14UD Pelletron Heavy Ion Accelerator at the Weizmann Institute in Rehovot. This "microscope" enables researchers to examine the atomic nucleus, one of the most minute and inscrutable structures in the entire universe.*

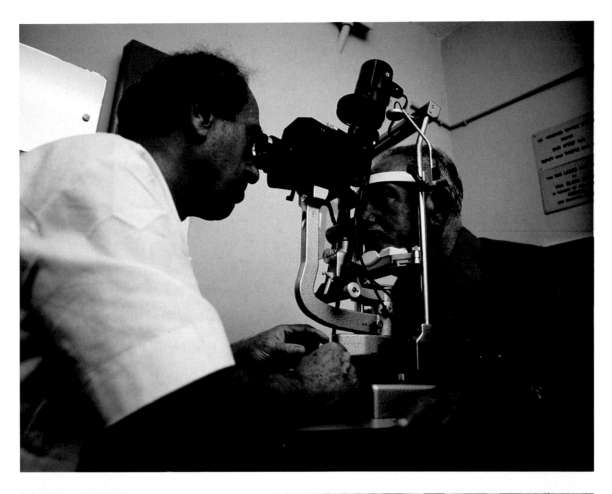

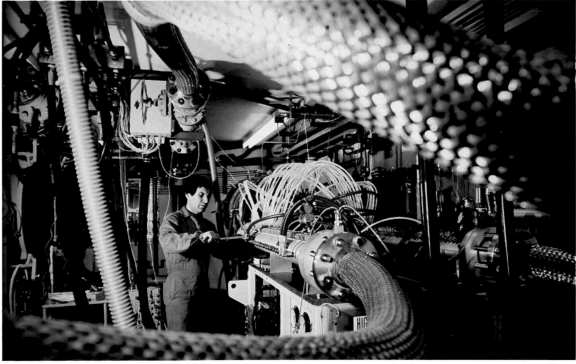

ABOVE: Performing
delicate laser micro-
surgery on the eye.
LEFT: A technician
services an arc plasma
generator at the
Technion in Haifa.

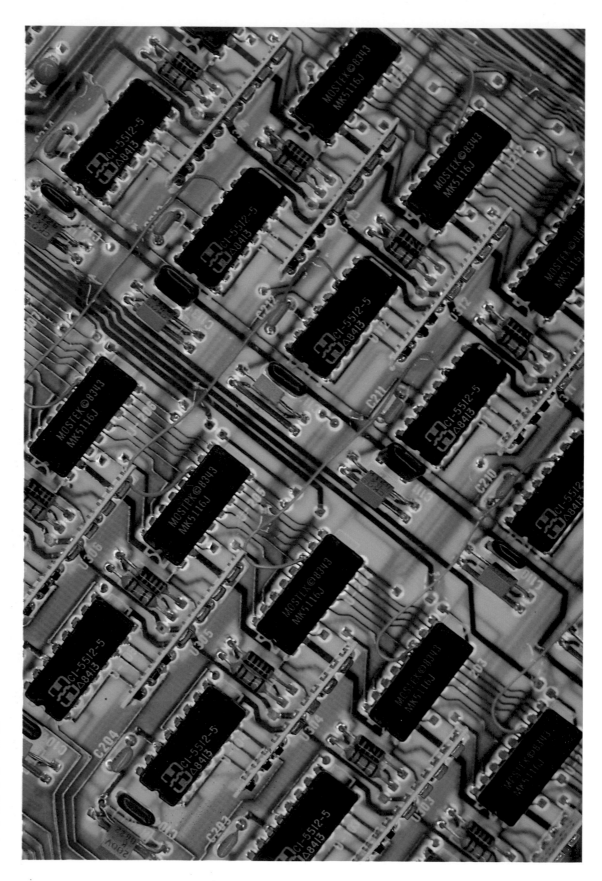

*Close-up of a printed circuit board with its various chips installed. It's part of a fiberoptics scanning system perfected by the Haifa firm of Fibronics. Israeli electronic technology has set new standards in many applied fields.*

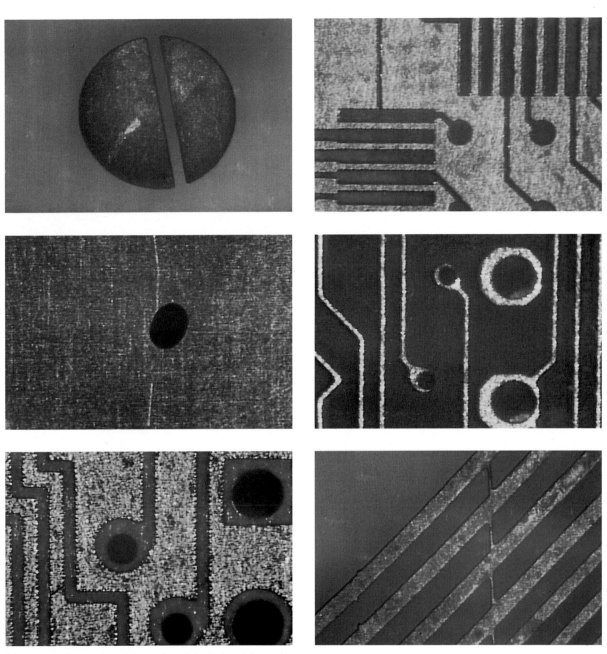

Macro photography of flaws in printed circuit boards. Optrotech has become a world leader in the field of error detection, evaluation and repair of PCBs. Here their VS-100 system has revealed specific flaws in six different PCBs. Look closely and see if you can find the short circuits, broken circuits, faulty chip connectors, inclusions, etc.

ABOVE: Solar collection panels in Sde Boker at the Institute for Desert Research. Private companies like Paz and Luz are also involved in this research; building their systems with components from the US, Germany and Japan. The IDR researches private systems in Sde Boker; if a system is successful and the Institute recommends it, the Israeli Ministry of Energy contributes 13% of the cost to build it in Israel.
RIGHT: Applied science for the masses: solar collectors generate storable power in daytime to light this remote bus stop at night near Qazrin in the Golan Heights. Such systems avoid the necessity of running in costly power lines.
OPPOSITE: The Schaefer Solar Furnace at the Weizmann Institute of Science. The Institute is a pioneer in solar research conducting experiments in solar ponds, light stimulated chemical reactions and solar lasers.

AN EXPRESSION OF SURVIVAL

*Israelis all...*

# Two Israelis: Three Opinions

YOU MIGHT CONSIDER ISRAEL AN OVER-burdened society, struggling under strong outside pressures from every angle you approach it," says Hebrew University Professor Moshe Lissak, perhaps the country's foremost expert on immigrant absorption. "There has always been a gap between available resources and immediate project needs." Even today, despite some $3 billion in US annual aid, the gap between resources and needs is an on-going problem that continues to shape Israeli society, some 4 million people from more than 70 different national origins.

The ever-present tensions in this melting pot go far to explain the old expression "two Israelis, three opinions," an inescapable fact of life in this over-stressed nation where everybody has something to say. Things were far simpler, however, in the early days of the Palestinian Yishuv. "Originally the Jews of Palestine were a very selective community," points out Professor Lissak. "Even under the Mandate there was very selective immigration. Priority was always given to the young Ashkenazim, those who could be easily mobilized for the building of a new society and not be a burden on the new state. Or permits were given to people with money and professional skills — like German Jews after Hitler took power."

Look, I was born here so I should know something about the place. My family was always a Labour Zionist clan," recalls Avraham Ben-Zvi, an agricultural machinery dealer from Haifa. "We built this country, and its roots were here long before 1948. My grandparents came in the Second Aliyah in 1906; from Minsk. My grandfather, he was a teacher, but here there was nobody to teach. They had nothing, so they had to work the land and scratch out their food. Then they tried to keep the Turks from stealing it from them.

"They always shared what little they had. In 1915 grandmother made Seder dinner for 14 people with two loaves and one fish. That was all she had to feed the people. She didn't even mind that her guests in-cluded three Sefardis from Egypt and an Armenian coppersmith — a Christian. In those days you shared with everybody because you believed you were building a better country. That was Eretz Yisrael the way it was when you had to support each other, when any friend was a treasure in a strange land."

"After the War of Independence, immigration had one of its most crucial periods," observes Professor Lissak. "New waves of immigration began in '49 — still in the midst of the war. The Israeli society of that time, composed of about 650,000 people, had to cope with two critical problems. One was the simple survival against the attacks of outside nations. The other problem was the absorption of masses of immigrants sufficient to double the population in four years.

"By 1959 about one million new Jews had immigrated. In the early years, about half of these new peoples came from Europe; the other half came from the Middle East. Beginning in the '60s, most of the new aliyot came from the Middle East. This was a huge task; even for a country of 50 million the rapid absorption of more than 600,000 would not be easy.

"So the first problem was simply logistic; one couldn't even deal as yet with social problems and services, with education. There were small groups of Jews concentrated in France and Italy, near port cities. These were survivors from the Nazi concentration camps. And there were also Jews in Cyprus, people deported by the British from Israel. Bringing in these people was the first mission.

"Then there were several other immediate tasks. Jews in Iraq and Yemen were in danger, followed by those from Libya and North Africa in general. Most of these peoples were now in danger from pogroms due to the frustration of the local Arabs at not being able to defeat Israel in the '48 War.

"After '48 a very different type of immigrant came. This greatly changed the demographic composition of the Jewish state, and the Sephardim would grow to about 55% of the population. Soon this became the cause of many racial problems.

"Those who came from Europe, survivors of the

Holocaust, had other problems of survival and adjustment. Many of them came in fragmented families. There were orphans, husbands without wives, wives without husbands. Obviously these people had other personal problems as well. Nevertheless their adjustment to Israeli society was much easier, much faster than that of the Oriental Jews. There was a common language for these people; nearly all of them spoke Yiddish, which had always been the language of communication in the Palestine Yishuv.

"Then the Moroccans came in two waves totalling about 250,000. For them immigration was only a half-immigration, and they were the problem children. Most Moroccan Jews came from the big cities; there they were the first generation to be exposed to the Western culture of the French. When they came to Israel, it was for them a regression, a tremendous trauma. They were often sent to the Negev or the Galil, not to Tel Aviv or centers of culture like the Casablanca they were accustomed to.

"Soviet Jews were confronted with other problems. Many of these 150,000 Russian immigrants were, in a sense, over-qualified. One of the greatest problems in Israel was that these diplomates were not trained to Western standards, so medical societies and the Government had to do fundamental re-education. Naturally many Soviet immigrants didn't like this; this meant downward mobility, at least for a couple of years."

If Jerusalem pastry shop owner Gershon Weissbrot is correct, Israel's Russian absorption problem will be a thing of the past. "Now the religious Right Wing want to see all of our brothers and sisters in Russia make a new aliyah, so they will have more Jews here to offset both the higher Arab birthrate and the secular influences of modern Israel. But what if they don't want to leave?" he asks rhetorically.

"Maybe now conditions under *peristroika* are not so bad for them. Maybe many are not Zionists but only wish to retain their Jewish identity in Soviet society. In Israel and also in America they are putting pressure on Gorbachev to let Jews emigrate, but if he let all the Jews leave, how many do you think would come here? I'll tell you, *habibi*, not very many. No, I think that most would elect to remain."

Israel's 70,000 Bedouin aren't immigrants, but their long record of loyalty to the State of Israel is exemplary — in sharp contrast to the often tenuous allegiance Israeli Arabs show for their State. Bedouin Sheikh Odeh Abu-Muammar, for example, was recently awarded the President's Citation for Volunteerism. For some 45 years he has inspired his large Negev tribe to aid the IDF in securing the borders; many of his people have served the army as trackers.

Tradition-bound and deeply religious Muslims, today Bedouin face inexorable social change while straining to keep enough of the old values to retain identity. "In the '60s the whole concept of schooling was alien to Bedouin culture," notes Aref Abu-Rabia, anthropologist at the Institute for Desert Research. "One of the strongest factors was the economic one; a child of eight is a valuable worker...But under the impact of modernization," he predicts, "it is clear that education will play a central role. The Bedouin themselves now wish their children to be educated," adds Abu-Rabia, himself a Bedouin.

Old habits are difficult to break, and many girls still drop out of school after grade 9. "They get married or they stay at home because their parents do not agree that they study in the same class as boys...but you have to modernize. You can't have electricity, running water and at the same time keep sheep and goats in a tent. This is the price they now pay," Abu-Rabia observes.

Bedouin are notably resourceful, even when it comes to applying contemporary law to salvage old traditions. "According to Muslim law a man may have up to four wives, but in 1957 the State of Israel forbade this," Abu-Rabia states. "However the Bedouin circumvent it because the Israeli law recognizes the rights of a mistress along with those of a lawful wife. So they figure that if this law is good for the Jews, it is also good for Bedouins. Now they take a second, third, even a fourth wife without registering them as wives, but as mistresses, who then have a right to a salary from the State!" he adds. "By now there are many of these cases...but I think only 2% have more than one wife."

The latest group of olim have perhaps been the most controversial of all: the Ethiopians, commonly termed "Falasha," although that term has slightly derogatory connotations for these handsome, dark-skinned people from the Horn of Africa. Shulamit Ben-Dor made aliyah nine years ago, and has since spent much of her time studying Ethiopians.

"There are now about 15,000 in Israel. Most were airlifted out via Sudan in Operation Moses from 1979-86...Approximately 15-20,000 still reside in Ethiopia — only half of the number who wanted to immigrate due to the border closing. We now know that many died en route to Israel," Ben-Dor adds sadly.

"Over 80% of them arrived illiterate, unprepared for a modern life in Israel. The average Ethiopian stayed in an absorption center for nearly 1½ years, training in Hebrew, modern living techniques (ie. plumbing, sanitation, etc.), along with vocational training."

Were the Ethiopians not so dark-skinned, their quiet ways might make them all but unnoticeable in contemporary Israel. Not so another immigrant group, whose outspoken views and blunt, often uncompromising politics put them regularly in the news. American-born Bob Steinberger is a contractor in Judea, and his ideas typify the rugged-individualist image the West Bank settlers there hold so dear. "The type of person who's going to change his life, to come to Israel, is not a wishy-washy person," notes the tough but affable Steinberger. "Then to come out here to the Gush, he's even less wishy-washy. Whether he's committed to the land or whether he's committed to the Yishuv, he's committed to building a new life and living up to its expectations.

"To tell the truth, before this whole intifada business started, I couldn't care less if you called me a settler or a townsperson. But now somebody says 'settler' and it's taken to mean a guy with a beard and a gun who goes out kickin' ass, beating everybody up. That's an unfortunate generalization."

Anybody who has visited the Gush Etzion settlements would probably agree. Certainly Rabbi Shlomo Riskin of Efrat resents comparison with the militant settlers of Kiryat Arba, some 25 kilometers to the south. "First off, you have to realize that the press has it wrong," opines Riskin as he tours his modern town on his bicycle. "This isn't a 'settlement,' it's a town. So you can see, we're not all gun-toters down here. We're building a new city."

With their Biblical claims behind them, Orthodox settlers in Judea are on the front line of conflict with local Arabs whether they like it or not. And they're a new breed of farmer.

"The first kibbutzniks in the Etzion Bloc were mostly Ashkenazim from Germany and Poland — secular Zionists who had escaped to Israel just before Hitler closed the doors," explains Shlomo Danziger of Kfar Etzion. "This particular kibbutz was liberated during the 1967 war, and it was partly rebuilt by the children of the original defenders in the '48 war. But most of these people didn't end up living here. Today we've got a new breed of kibbutznik. Our new Zionists are observant Jews, not secular like the old ones. They've got too much invested in the Gush, and they don't believe in trading land for peace with the Palestinians."

If there is one socio-political touchstone for the West Bank settlers, it is the movement known as Gush Emunim, literally "Bloc of the Faithful." Rabbi Menachem Fruman of Tekoa explains how the movement started: "Gush Emunim was formed in 1974 by students of Rabbi Zvi Yehuda Kook. It was formed not as a political but as a social movement, and one of its social aims was to get closer relations between religious and non-religious Jews in Israel.

"Now while some settlements have been established against government decisions not to settle certain parts of the West Bank, the principle of Gush Emunim was to force the government and then have the public support the action. We feel that we are the missionaries of the national will.

"We would never sacrifice Judea, Samaria and Gaza for an acceptable solution with the Palestinians," declares Fruman with the finality of ultimate conviction. "The Zionist idea is to settle the land of Israel and that includes the West Bank and Gaza. Giving up the West Bank is like a husband who is willing to let his wife hang around with other men for the reason of improving the relationships between them."

Retention of the land is sacrosanct for Gush people, so when Herutniks and right-wingers in general hear some public figure suggest that the Palestinians be given their own slice of the West Bank, their reactions are predictably explosive:

"Look at that son-of-a-bitch Ori Orr!" exclaims automobile dealer Baruch Yarden from Ashkelon. "He spends a lifetime in the army [former chief of Northern Command] fighting the goddam Arabs. Now he resigns, joins the Labour party, and sounds off about giving half the country back to the same people who have been shooting at his ass all these years. He's a traitor to the security of the nation!

"If, God forbid, Labour wins the next election, we'll have war with the Arabs within a year. Why? Because they'll know for sure that we're divided and weak.

"It's insane," Yarden exclaims, waving his hands in the air. "Do you have any retired generals in America who wish to hand over all the states west of the Mississippi to the Vietnamese?"

There's people who say the Arabs should be sent away, that's the extremist opinion of Rabbi Kahane. But not all the Arabs are bad, you know," baker Martin Fisher of Efrat observes. "I disagree entirely with Meir Kahane; it's just not right to give them a one-way ticket out of Israel. Extremist opinion, I think, is mostly among the young, the yeshiva people who come here from the States. I think they've been brainwashed with this Kehane stuff."

For those who have come face-to-face with the violence of the intifada, however, opinions are usually more polarized. "As far as I'm concerned, the set-tlers can do anything without any blame at all," declares pizza-maker Harvey Dan of Efrat. "If they don't get any protection, then they've gotta do it themselves....A while ago I heard on the news that one Arab was killed and six wounded. I said 'Damn! Why not the other way around. Why not six dead and one wounded?' And that's not like me at all."

"The basic problem is that we have two people fighting over the same land," explains Bob Steinberger. "God forbid there should be a Palestinian state here. Here there's absolutely no industry, no money. The only way it could exist is for the Russians or somebody to support it. And then we'd have an unstable Cuba in the Middle East."

"The Arabs ought to get their West Bank state, but if we gave it to them, they'd all have guns overnight and we would have no security," proclaims Jerusalem's Ezra Gordesky, a museum curator. "It's true of all hot climate peoples — you just can't trust them. I was in Cairo for a month on a job recently. There they all lie. The government lies to the people; the people lie to themselves. It's all lies with the Arabs, and they don't even trust themselves."

Leave the West Bank, and rural attitudes about the Arabs are noticeably more equivocal. Egyptian-born Esther Nehab and her Sabra husband Etan live on the seacoast at Kibbutz Nasholim. As with many families, the Arab situation has split the household.

"We're not very religious here at Nasholim, but we are Israelis and something has to be done to solve our problems today," states Esther. "The Arabs ought to have some rights...until they interfere with our own, of course. There's nothing in the Bible that says we have to treat other people as slaves. We have rights to this country, but so do they."

"I have much stronger feelings," responds Etan. "I don't like Shamir because he just does so many things without reason. But yes, I'm what you call a strong Herutnik, and I don't think we should trade territory for a temporary peace. Look, the way you have to negotiate with the Arabs is to show them you're strong.

The minute they think you're weak and divided, that's when they attack you.

"I think we should give all the Arabs full citizenship," Etan continues, "but before that we should re-arrange the voting patterns so that the Arab districts are big enough so that they will never have enough Knesset members to control. That's the only way Israel can stay a Jewish state — which it was meant to be."

"We cannot ignore the existence of Arabs in Israel. We must live together, and I believe we can," says Rabbi Fruman. "I have a hypothetical idea of two nations living on the same piece of land with two different leaderships. Even though such an idea does not exist in any state as yet, I believe it is possible."

West Jerusalem jewelry store owner Shaul Ben Shlomo has similar thoughts. "Look, American Jews live in a Christian state. They do not complain now that they are assimilated. So why can't the Arabs live here in a Jewish state and be likewise assimilated?"

But some people balk at extending full citizenship to West Bank Arabs. For them, survival comes before democracy. "I've got nothing against giving Arabs in the West Bank full citizenship; just like Arabs in Israel proper," says Bob Steinberger. "But I've got a problem. I really believe this must be a Jewish state....give them another 20 years, and they're gonna out-vote me. What they couldn't do in war, they'll do in parliament.

"So they don't vote. If you say to me that's immoral, I say you're right. If you say to me that's undemocratic, I say you're right. But the problem is I gotta survive. If this became a completely democratic state....we wouldn't have a Jewish state."

Others feel that prior Arab malfeasance has somehow abrogated the rights of today's Palestinians. "During the Jordanian occupation, they uprooted half the graves up on the Mount of Olives cemetery, where they put in a road," points out Rabbi Porush. "And where my grandfather is buried, they uprooted half the cemetery and used the tomb stones to pave their army camps...I hope that when the world will have to decide something about Israel, it will remember our

behavior and the behavior of the Arabs."

"My mother, she lives in St. Louis. One time two months ago she came to visit us here in Israel," recalls Herzliya accountant Shmuel Eskanizi. "She read the papers, saw the television, so she wanted to see the West Bank for herself. We took her to Beita, where that little girl was killed. We were there for only an hour and already she wants to leave. 'Not since I was a little girl in Smolensk have I seen so many men with guns,' she says. 'What kind of place is this, Shmuel? They have traded the Cossacks for the settlers. It's *m'shuggeh* and now I want to go back to America where even the *goyim* don't play games like this.'

"So what could I say to her? She's 82 and she's seen enough guns for 100 lifetimes."

Since he left his native Italy in 1968, refrigeration engineer Mose Benvenisti from Haifa has made a hobby of keeping track of Palestinian groups:

"To begin with, Jews in Palestine have only rarely been able to identify their adversaries, to pin-point just who is in control of the Arab uprisings against them. People tend to forget that political fragmentation among the Arabs has been one of the biggest causes of trouble in Palestine.

"Nowadays when you read of a terrorist act against Israelis, it's always assumed that the PLO is behind it. Many times it has been the PLO, but it is incorrect to assume there is only one PLO organization, and that all PLO activities are under Arafat's control.

"Shamir was a cretin when he so much as admitted that Israelis were behind the assassination of Abu Jihad in Tunisia. As an old Mossad agent himself he should have known that there were other, non-Arafat, Palestinian organizations who wanted to kill Abu Jihad. He could just as easily have blamed them for the job. Even when Arafat takes a moderate position, other groups oppose it and start more troubles.

"Before Independence, the Egyptians, the Iraqis, the Jordanians and the Grand Mufti all promoted violence against Jews. After the war each took turns trying to establish itself as the leading controller of the Palestinians in the refugee camps and among the Israeli Arabs. Caught in the middle were the Palestinians themselves. They've never been able to select their own leaders for themselves. Even when they have democratic elections in the West Bank, the PLO calls for boycott because they are under Israeli supervision.

"These days the trouble is that the Western press thinks all 'Abus' are created equally and all are one and the same. They're not. 'Abu' simply means 'father' in Arabic, and many Palestinians have taken it as a nom de guerre. Arafat is Abu Amar, or 'father of the revolution;' Abu Nidal broke with Arafat years ago, and in the meantime his group has been responsible for so many car bombings you cannot imagine. And the *Achille Lauro*. His group wounded the Israeli ambassador in London in 1982.

"There is also Abu Maizer. His group is based in Damascus, and these fellows hijacked that Egyptian airliner in Malta. The list is also much longer. There is Abu Mousa, who fought Arafat in Lebanon; Nayev Hawatmeh's Democratic Front for the Liberation of Palestine; George Habash and his Damascus gang of criminals are called the Popular Front for the Liberation of Palestine; and so on. From time to time each of these gangs passes under the control of outsiders like Assad, Khomeni, Khadaffi. Then you add in the Syrian-backed Amal militia in Lebanon, the Iran-backed Hizbullah in Lebanon and you have a real mix-up. Any one of them could have killed Abu Jihad; any one of them could stage a terrorist operation against Israel tomorrow. What a mess! There will not be peace for Israel until all of them are either eliminated or satisfied."

**P**alestinians will never pick a leader other than Arafat," predicts Jerusalem barman Abu Dahoud. "Yes, I know you think he has done many bad things, and he has. But his whole life has been spent in the Palestinian cause. He doesn't have a goddam thing but the jacket on his back; he has no home; he lives in Tunisia — for now....Of course we cannot eat guns, but our people are determined to fight for generations. The Israelis, you know, have given us an example — Begin.

He was a terrorist, but he became Prime Minister and then the world recognized him.

"Americans have heroes. English have heroes. Jews have heroes. *We* have no scientists, no astronauts, no sports heroes your newspapers are full of," laments Abu Dahoud. "Palestinians have no heroes, nobody in the news unless somebody is killing or hijacking. Yes, I confess such persons are bad heroes for our children, very bad, but they are the only ones Palestinians see risking their lives to fight for rights."

The majority of the Palestinians are willing to live in peace with the State of Israel, but they want to have their own privilege to decide their future for themselves," observes Teddy Kollek's East Jerusalem Advisor Amir Cheshin. "But Palestinians think they're the underdogs. Underdogs not only as seen by Israel and the Americans, but by the Arab states themselves."

**L**ast May, IDF troops spent three days in southern Lebanon in an effort to eradicate terrorist strongholds. Some 400 suspected terrorists were killed, but not all Israelis agreed with the efficacy of the operation, suggesting there are alternative methods.

"I think maybe it is not so good we go into the Lebanon with our army to punish the Hizbullah and the Amal terrorists. That is why I do not like Shamir. He is a little man and always he tries to be Napoleon with guns and beatings just to show how strong he is," says Elazar Litani, an appliance store owner from Haifa.

"Listen, our Mossad has already done more damage to the Hizbullah and the Amal than a three-day army adventure ever could. Yes, you may believe it that our Mossad people have faked their way into these groups in the Lebanon, and they have succeeded in making them fight each other. Look! They are bombing and shooting themselves now. This is a cheap way to defeat our enemies, is it not?"

**I**'m only half-Palestinian. My mother came from Egypt to marry my father when she was sixteen years. I think that was about 1951, and it was not easy for an Arab to move to Israel then," remembers Haji

Sinora, owner of a Jerusalem falafel restaurant. "My father has always lived in Haifa. He was one of the few — very few — Arabs not to leave his house when war came in 1948.

"He always told his children that the last thing they should give up was their land. 'Tell the people with power anything that will please them,' he said, 'and say anything to keep your land.'

"At that moment, most of his friends believed what the Jordanians and the Egyptians told them: they would get their houses back and more when all the Jews had been killed. But my father did not believe them. He had always good relations with Jews. When the war came no Jew ever told my father to leave his house. So he stayed in his place, and now he has four houses, and people are renting from him.

"So what does this mean? That Arabs and Jews get along? Not all the time, my friend. No, because there are many cruel people who do not wish for peace on any conditions except their own. Maybe some new leaders will come who will honestly believe we are all Palestinians and give everybody the same rights. But I do not think that will be soon. No, first there will be war. And many people will die because foolish leaders must make big demonstrations of hate; they think that is the way they keep control over the people."

I f the Israelis offered the West Bank Palestinians full citizenship I think many would accept that," says Jerusalem camel driver Khalil Naihmi. "You don't know how difficult it is to be less than second class because you are Arab. We have no voting, no civilian justice. But most important we have no opportunity to advance. Our people are much better under the Israelis than they ever would be under Jordanians — who in any case were always lousy bastards to the Palestinian people," a Sherut driver from Issawaya Village acknowledges. "The problem starts when we realize that we have not our own country. Most Palestinians are not happy with this, but they would not risk their work to revolt and perhaps get something much less. The problem is our leaders. They think that they will

not stay long unless they lead us into revolution."

"Yes, I think it [Jewish rule] is better economically for the Palestinian people, but our leaders are not always happy to see us working in peace with the Israelis. Many times our people are throwing stones at the soldiers because they are required to do so," reflects Marwan Abdullah, custodian at the Monastery of the Temptation. "And then there is trouble, people are killed and there is even more anger. Here I work for the Christian monks, so it is very different for me. And I myself am a believer.

"But I am still a Palestinian, and you must write that there should be a settlement here to avoid more bloodshed. And you must look at these refugee camps. You have seen them? There are three of them here close to Jericho. Some people have been living there for forty years, and they cannot afford to move anywhere else. Many came from cities like Jaffa and Haifa, and of course they wish to return home. However nobody wants them. Not the Israelis, not the Arab countries. Only the United Nations gives them some food, I think, but it is not very much. So there is much hatred, much anger. Our people condemn the Israelis, but I think it is not only the Israelis who should be condemned."

C ertainly many Israelis are ready to slap a share of the blame on the United Nations, about which few have anything good to say.

"Those UNRWA refugee camps are a mess. They're a political showpiece where even the Israeli government has no power to do anything," lambastes Erika Nordig, mother of three and a Jerusalem travel agent. "With all their money, do you think the other Arab states are interested in the welfare of the Palestinians? Of course not. They don't give them any money, they don't offer to take in some of these poor people. No, they want to keep them here living in the worst kind of poverty so they can use them to embarrass Israel.

"I can't think of anything positive that the presence of UN troops has accomplished since the 1973 war. They live a fine life here with their fancy cars...many just spend their time drinking, and some even do drug smuggling because they know they'll never get caught with their diplomatic status. Here the UN just spends a lot of money but doesn't do anything for the people they're supposed to be helping."

Prime Minister Yitzhak Shamir has had to shoulder an undue share of the blame for the failure of the Schultz mission, when in fact the plan was fatally flawed from the start. "There are many Palestinians who are blaming Reagan and Schultz for some of the present troubles," says Ibrahim Mansour with a note of rancor. "It is not because we hate Americans. No, we like them because there is real democracy for all peoples — not just whites. No, Mr. Schultz angered our people when he went to Jordan to talk with Hussein. So it is then appearing that America and Israel are trying to give us away to Jordan.

"You will not believe me, but it is correct that more Palestinians have died from Jordanian machine guns than from Israeli. Hussein is only a playboy. I have heard your people say that the Arab countries with oil give no money to the Palestinians. That is not exactly true. Every year millions are sent through Jordan for our people, but they do not get to us. Jordanians steal it. How else can they pay for all their new buildings?

"So you can now perhaps understand why we are angered when Mr. Schultz is talking to Jordan. They do not want us, and we do not want them. We dislike them even more than the Israelis of Shamir."

So you write a book. About which people? Arabs or Jews? About Israel? Then if you are truthful you will write that things are bad here, very bad for the Arab people since 1967. The goddam Jews, they are the problem. Why don't they just get out and leave us alone?" asks East Jerusalem flower seller Mahmoud. "Here they treat us like animals; always they are asking for passport, identity cards. You drive on the road, goddam Jews, they stop you if your number plate on the car is blue. So that is Jewish democracy?

"You like my flowers, I think. Yes, the Iris are very beautiful, very beautiful. No, we do not grow them ourselves. They grow them near Beersheba. People from India, I think. They are saying these people are goddam Jews also, but that is only more lies. My brother told me they are goddam Hindus, and what my brother says is always correct."

Notwithstanding the heated emotions of most Palestinians, there are those who would relegate the Arab-Israeli conflict to something less than their first concern. "Right now our biggest problem is the division between Israelis and Jews. You expected me to say our problems started and finished with the Arabs? I am sorry to disappoint you, but we would have almost no trouble here in Israel if our Jews were only of one flavor," Jerusalem Pharmacist Yehuda Aretz says flatly.

Hand in glove with the Jew vs. Israeli conflict goes the inescapable fact that society itself has changed its values since the days of the Yishuv. "In forty years people have become more individual. There is an increase in self-actualization, less interest in collective goals. There's more religion and capitalism today," notes psychology professor Amia Lieblich. "Fewer people exist for the State than vice-versa, almost the opposite of what things were."

But one doesn't hear academic definitions on the street. There, in the bustle of modern Israel, the common man fights the Jew vs. Israeli battle with a caustic rhetoric. "Today yeshivas are very popular, and many of those kids who don't qualify are still written in on the roles in order to escape the army," declares Jerusalemite Yigael Sheretz. "Little bastards! When I was sweating my ass off in the Yom Kippur war, these guys and their rabbis were scared to death the Arabs would come in and cut off their *peyot!*

"Look, write your book anyway you choose, but if you want Israelis — most Israelis anyway — to believe it, tell them that the goddam Orthodox have stolen this country away from the rest of us Jews!

"When we — and I'm talking about Israelis — are drafted into the army, some of us get our first taste of what it means to be a Jew in Israel," says Shmuel Eskenazi. "Our chaplains tell us what we have to eat how we must observe Shabbat. If we have problems with our wives and girlfriends, if our parents die or divorce, the chaplains don't wish to know about it."

"Do you know my village and its big yeshiva?" asks a hitch-hiking IDF sergeant from Alon Shevut in Gush Etzion. "Listen, I was raised in that place, where the *Halacha* is everything, and where the local rabbis have their own interpretation of God. The Gush people are mostly new arrivals in Israel; now they're telling all the old people from the early aliyot what to do.

"I am one of the few who rebelled; that's why I'm thinking of making a career out of the army. Of course we have bullshit regulations and all that, but at least in the army you can think. Except when you're on duty in the Occupied Territories, and then you think only of saving yourself by keeping out of trouble.

"Look, one day I came home from Haifa with some army friends — on leave. When my parents came in at the end of the day, they started right in on my army comrades. 'What? You don't observe Shabbat? You eat unclean food? What is the army doing to its people? It's bad enough Rabin has you beating the Arabs, but have you forgotten what country you live in?' My mother was very angry with them, and she tried to make them feel ashamed about their poor attention to Jewish Law.

"Finally one of them lost his patience with her. 'Can't you see that our — your — blessed *Halacha* is tearing this country apart? My grandfather was at Tel Hai with Trumpeldor. His sweat and his rifle built his village, built this country as a place of true democratic opportunity. Today his son, my father, intends to keep it that way. And so does his grandson!'

"Of course my mother was very shocked. You don't usually speak to religious people like that — at least not in the Gush. So my friend excused himself and left for the bus stop. At the door he turned to my parents, 'If I leave the army I think I will become a pig farmer. I have developed a taste for white steak, anyway!'"

**F**ar from the bickering of the cities, far from the West Bank is the Golan, where one is likely to find three Golanis with perhaps only one opinion.

"I don't know why more people don't want to move here. Or why more tourists don't come," muses a young petrol station attendant in Qazrin. "It's really a beautiful land, much easier to farm and raise animals than in that rock-filled West Bank — especially Judea....And there's not a large group of Arab population to fight with," she adds.

"But perhaps it is better that Arik Sharon and those Gush Emunim people never wanted to make settlements here. Yes, I think it is better because those people make too much trouble wherever they are. In any case, we don't need a load of yeshivas up here, with their rabbis telling us what to do all of the time."

"I have four Arab workers from the nearby village of Iksal. I'm the only Jew," declares goose farmer Odet Denebom from Moshav Tel Adiqim, near Nazareth. "But we get along well because we have to spend so much time together. There is no problem here in the North. We have become good friends; they come to my house and I go to theirs in Iksal. The problem is in the Occupied Areas like the West Bank and Gaza; there they live under military law and it's different. There really is no solution to the problem because we want to stay here and so do the Arabs. We must learn to live together in the same place," admits Denebom.

"A man named Aful lives in this moshav. He is a Right Wing activist. Many of the younger people are following him; they will not give the Arabs the West Bank and want to kick them out. I don't think it's good that so many young people listen to him," opines Denebom. "There will always be people at the opposite extremes, but they don't speak for everyone. Most people just want to live their lives."

**Y**ou have your own problems in the United States. What's going to happen when Jesse Jackson doesn't get the nomination? Just like the Palestinians. There's going to be large groups of ignorant blacks who are going to show their anger by rioting. It could be troubles just like the West Bank," says museum curator Ezra Gordesky in a feisty manner. "So...you have your crime, too, in the United States. And your government corruption. Even with Jewish people. Now we have the same thing here. Look what it says here in the paper about Israeli crime — 'a blight unto the nations!' "

American aid is something most Israelis can live with, although it carries an obvious diplomatic price. Apparently some people feel there has been a social price as well. "Yes, everybody in Israel is very grateful for all the money our country receives from the United States. In the 1973 war, for example, Americans made it possible for Israel to survive. Yes, it was very close to extermination for our country. But perhaps now that our opponents are not so strong and are deeply divided, perhaps now it is time for America to stop giving money," says IDF Captain Eliyahu Revat.

"Of course this money has made life easier for Israelis to deal with the Arabs — but it has also made it easier for Israelis to be lazier with their own society.

"Yes, life is comfortable here, but it is also very expensive to be very comfortable. Perhaps if we Israelis were not so comfortable then we would return to the old values where there was harder work, less stealing from each other and the government. Today things are too easy. Now we have a 47-hour work week, but practically no person works 47 hours. I think it is more like 30 hours left after long lunches, coffeebreaks, listening to the radio, telephoning our girlfriends, taking time off for shopping, going to the bank and things like that," details Captain Revat.

For all its immigrant successes, Israel has not been a happy experience for *all* its citizens. "Emigration is a great distress to our society and everyone is embarrassed to speak about it," confesses Professor Lissak. "Still, from every immigrant country there is emigration. You can't imagine how many left the United States at the beginning of the 19th Century. Every absorptive society has its opposites, but in Israel it's very different because of how people here feel.

"As a society we all blame each other. If newcomers leave after one or two years, we can swallow it because we know ours is a very tense society and the adjustment is difficult. The big problem is when the Sabras leave, especially when they are children of the elite. We now have Sabra representatives in the Diaspora in the USA; they form a group we call the Yordim, or 'those who have gone down.' It's a natural disaster you can't do anything about."

"Sure, I admit I came over here with ideas of making aliyah. You know in America, Jews are really only an assimilated minority in a predominantly Christian country. Here it's different. I like it — that's why I'm back here on vacation. But I didn't like it enough to stay," says Leo Bernstein, a former kibbutznik in Carmiel, who returned to New York after three years.

"Look, most Jews in the States come from Reform temples. Our people there contribute the lion's share of the money to Jewish welfare organizations. They think they're doing their part for Israel, the sort of religious motherland. They think they're buying a piece of the home team, but when they come over here and really see what their status is, they realize, like I did, that there's absolutely no way they'll ever be a fully accepted part of that home team.

"And here's the Jewish Agency with its hand out all over the Diaspora, fund-raising for an Israel that religiously cuts out most of its contributors. Now elections are coming, so Shamir and Peres are in New York to get money. They will raise millions, and when they come back home the government will give them more. I read somewhere that they will spend about $14 million apiece. Unbelievable in this tiny country where they cannot even afford to fix the roads properly! It's *m'shuggeh*, that's what it all is."

I'm tired of hearing American Jews tear into our government from the comforts of their big homes and fat incomes. They talk about democracy, philosophy and all that crap," exclaims airport administrator Reuben Hadar.

"Sure, they send us money; after all, Israel gives them another team to cheer for, another source of entertainment where they can actually buy their way into ownership and get a plaque to prove it.

"This country was built by people like my parents,

who came here with nothing, and worked six days a week to scratch out a living in the '30s. We know what real sacrifice is. Those kids they send over to make Bar Mitzvah have no idea what made this country great. If they like it so much over here, why don't they make aliyah?" asks Hadar bitterly.

"Look, Americans make good raw material for the Zionist state — that's really why I would like to see more come over. Better some spoiled Americans than some more dirty Russians or Moroccans who would rather go to New York anyway. But Americans make very poor judges. Listen, they have so many secular, assimilated Jews they don't know who to follow. I read somewhere lately that American Jews need Israel for their healthy Jewish identity. If they want that so much, how come so many changed their names to some goyishe-sounding abomination?"

**F**or an increasing number of contemporary Israelis, Orthodoxy plays a pre-eminent role; the scriptures are used as guidelines for life, and caveats for those who would dare challenge the country and its policies. "The Bible tells us that the enemies of Israel will be punished 'measure for measure,' and that's just what happened," remarks Bob Sigal, fund-raiser for an Orthodox Jerusalem girls' orphanage.

"Look at history. Every empire that has sought to divide Israel has fallen on evil times. Look at the Assyrians, the Babylonians, the Romans, the Ottomans. All of them. Back in the '20s the British Empire was at its height. Then they put Abdullah and Faisal on the thrones of Transjordan and Iraq, put the Jew-hating, pro-Nazi Grand Mufti in office here in Jerusalem. The first people the British killed after the Second World War began in 1939 were not Germans; they were Jews trying to immigrate to Palestine. Within only 30 years the British Empire was finished. The Chernobyl disaster was most certainly God's punishment on the Soviet Union for their cruel treatment of the Jews. And you'll see that if the United States ends up supporting the wrong side over here, then they, too, will be punished measure for measure."

**T**he roots of Secular-Orthodox political polarization probably go back to the late '40s, when Ben-Gurion made concessions to religious parties whose help he needed in coalitions. As both politician and son of an Agudat Party MK, Rabbi Porush well remembers that Mapai's discrimination paved the way for much of Menachem Begin's success.

"Mapai's attitude towards the Jews of North Africa created a feeling of discontent, discrimination against the Sefardi community. Begin, who was in the opposition at this time, was trying to gain power, and he recognized how Ben-Gurion's behavior made the Sefardi communities feel inferior. So discrimination was what gave Begin his hook.

"The truth is that Mapai prepared the foundations for the religious communities of today. Yeshiva students who want to study the Torah don't have to serve in the army. Religious girls don't have to serve in the army. But once Mapai became more stable, they started to forget their supporters.

"When Begin was Prime Minister for seven years, the Likud had more special sensitivities to religious issues. Religious representatives were successful in amending certain laws, achieving their policies through coalition agreements or discussions with national leaders."

**I**f indeed Israel is "a nation like any other," then it is also unlike any other. When the early Zionist fathers successfully developed the agrarian socialist society which came to be known as the Kibbutz Movement, they created a socio/political organism which is alive with continually renewed vitality nearly 80 years after the first kibbutz was founded at Degania. By the time of the '48 War, the Kibbutz Movement had become something of a national backbone.

"In 1942 the first news of the Holocaust came to Palestine; now people were quite sure that a disaster was underway, and only then did Jewish leaders begin to think of bringing in endangered Jews from wherever they were in trouble," recalls Professor Moshe Lissak. "Jews were also in difficulty in Iraq, and there were also ideas of starting selective immigration for young Iraqis.

In those days, of course, there was no legal immigration from Iraq, and often young girls were brought in illegally. This was the first shift in planned assimilation to include Oriental Jews, but it didn't last very long. There was strong resistance among the Iraqi Jews at giving up only their children.

"The initiative for this selective immigration came from the Kibbutz Movement, with strong support from Ben-Gurion. The Kibbutz Movement had always been very active in the preparation of Jews from Europe, and now they sent five or six people to Iraq to organize underground protection for the Jews there following several ugly incidents. They established a Haganah there, and this was the forerunner of youth movements and Zionist indoctrination," Lissak continues.

"Ironically, after '48 the Kibbutz Movement played a very minor role in the absorption of immigrants. Many kibbutzniks were very active as individuals, but as a movement they became very selective in the absorption of new immigrants. And the reasons were logistical. First of all, it's not easy to absorb a family of 7 or 8 into a kibbutz, especially a family that has no understanding of or wish to remain in a kibbutz atmosphere. To live in a kibbutz is a radical revolution for those not accustomed to it. Those who came from the Middle East had no such an idea of a communal organization; it was as though they were on the moon!

"Their greatest contribution during the Wars of Independence was that they took in thousands of children for education. Many new immigrants in shanty towns couldn't afford to have their small children with them nor could they give them education, so the children were sent to kibbutz youth groups.

"By the end of the '60s the new immigrants were more or less absorbed into the labor market. Unemployment was now very low, whereas in the beginning it had reached nearly 25%. In the '60s the rate of economic growth was one of the highest in the world reaching as high as 10%. I don't think that even Japan achieved this rate of growth. This was one of Israel's real success stories, and it facilitated the absorption of the immigrants. Without this rate of growth, of course,

such a large number of people could not have been absorbed. The combination of money and manpower was the key to Israel's economic success."

Throughout the social history of Eretz Yisrael the greatest unifier has been the military. With universal conscription for both men and women — with the exception of several thousand yeshiva students — the IDF is the mold through which everybody must pass. "I was in the army with a large group of exclusively immigrants. They were from Persia, from Argentina, Portugal, Ethiopia, England, America....One guy was even from Sri Lanka," notes Martin Fisher, a baker who made aliyah from England. "Being in the army and having to help each other sort of built up harmony between all the small elements of society isn't always easy. You can't force everyone to be religious, so there's a mild friction between the various groups...especially the ultra-Orthodox who don't serve in the army. There's a lot of non-religious in the army. On the most important fast day, Yom Kippur, there were quite a lot of soldiers who were eating. And they were saying to me, 'Why aren't you eating?' And I told them, 'It's only the army. I've always fasted on Yom Kippur, and I'm not stopping now.'"

Fisher immigrated because "it was very difficult to find work with days off on Saturdays." In contrast to the Orthodoxy displayed by many new arrivals, most of the older kibbutzniks have remained distinctly secular. While many had strong political ties, most paid little heed to the *Halacha*. At Kibbutz Nasholim, Egyptian-born Esther Nehab will tell you, "We have most of everything we need...you know everybody, you know where almost everybody is, so if you need help, it's always there. We're an extended family."

And this chatty mother of three is also very frank about *kashrut*, observed in the dining hall, more as a courtesy than an obligation, but in few of the kibbutznik's homes. "Of course our kibbutz is supposed to be kosher. We have to be kosher in order to be able to sell our produce through the regional food cooperatives.

But there's always a way around things.

"Every year the rabbi comes to inspect us and approve our operation. We pay him for his services, and we sometimes have to pay him also under the table. Some years ago we wanted to raise pigs. For the rabbi we called them 'ducks;' we paid him off and things were okay. I mean, that's how they get their money anyway."

For those not living on collectives, life is substantially less tranquil. The intifada has jeopardized the regular employment of many Arabs, as the uprising dictates opening and closing times to a cowed populace. Bob Steinberger tells a story related to him by an Arab construction worker in Tekoa: "Another worker told me about his friend, and why the present troubles just can't go on. The other day the PLO guys came around to his house and wanted to know why his son was missing from the local demonstration. He said he didn't know, but then he sent him away to a friend's house in another town. The next day the PLO goons returned. 'Where's your son?' 'I don't know,' said the man. So they broke both his arms."

Israel's three municipalities have much in common with most other Western cities, where the groaning bureaucracies leave nearly everybody incensed.

"Our problems begin with our bureaucracies; people who are lazy and careless leave our citizens very angry when they must wait months — years — for a simple transaction," bemoans Belgian immigrant Aaron Getzler. "Our civil servants put our people through hell, and many of our private organizations are guilty also.

"Sometimes I think we Israelis take out vengeance on each other with paperwork. The mentality, it's like this: I must wait forever for your office to process my forms, so I'm going to make you wait forever when I handle yours. Government agencies are all over-staffed with people who got their jobs because they had *protekzia*. The more people who are hired, the less work is actually done," declares travel agent Getzler, thumping his office countertop for emphasis.

Certainly bank clerk Yaacov Ben-Yamini from Tel Aviv agrees. "Nu, have you had to use an Israeli bank lately? Yes? Then you know that our system is a mess. Here there are times you need to visit no less than three different counters to cash a check. And have you noticed that many counters are open while the employees behind them drink their coffee or talk on the telephone?" asks this Jerusalem-born Sabra. "Our workers' respect for their jobs has deteriorated; they don't care. They get paid every week and the bank can never fire them with all the regulations.

"I am not too old to have forgotten the spirit in the land during the War of Independence. Ah, yes," Ben-Yamini pauses to shift his gaze heavenward, "those were wonderful times; daily emergencies made heroes out of us all. Perhaps today America should give no more money to Israel for a while. Surely our standard of living would go down, but our standard of work and behavior would perhaps go back up."

Older people are invariably quicker to point out the changes in urban work ethics; many are distinctly unhappy. Ezra Gordesky came from London to find a better world; after many years he's not always sure he's succeeded. "See all those people sitting with their coffee on Ben Yehuda Street? They're not just tourists, they're workers who are taking time off from their jobs. They've lost their pride in the State. All they want is their paychecks from the bureaucracy," he sums up.

"Many of us still behave like Third World people. We throw our garbage into someone else's yard or out into the streets. We've also got 1½ million lower class citizens whom we rule over largely because their leaders are even more divided than ours. By those definitions, that's not a basis for calling us a First World nation despite all of our military technology," laments Jerusalem accountant Miriam Mendes.

Yale University graduate Bob Sigal sees the reasons behind much of today's social disquietude as having irreligious roots: "Most people have failed to look at Israel from a religious perspective. Today's education has so stressed how to make a living that people are no longer interested in the philosophical questions of what makes man happy. Or how he should live in order to enjoy a productive life."

In the early days of nationhood, when danger to the State was greater and Zionist society was much more homogeneous, Israelis acquiesced to hardship much better than they do today. Ironically, some people see the bureaucracies that built the country as now strangling it and running costs through the roof.

"Look at these prices! Chicken is now up over 20%. Overnight! Because the government has decided to lower the subsidy on many foods, just like that. Now the shopkeepers are getting crazy because they cannot get rid of their stock at the new prices although they will now have to pay more for replacement," complains Yossi Ben-Eliezer, a salesman from Petach Tikvah. "Now if the government are not careful there will be another explosion of inflation."

Israel's avowedly export-oriented economy may succeed in earning invaluable foreign exchange, but every time there are price increases, especially in foodstuffs, locals feel they're getting the short end of the stick. "Now my boy, I'm going to take you around this market and show you how Israeli agricultural progress has made the exporters fortunes and us local consumers poor people," declares housewife Ruth Shalev.

"Look at these tomatoes. Eight shekels fifty a kilo! An entirely crazy price when they are grown no more than thirty kilometers away. My son has friends who grow them — in greenhouses. They are very good, as you can see, and they stay fresh for more than a month," she comments with a mixture of pride and bitterness. "But these tomatoes are so good that the markets can hoard them until the prices go up, and with the intifada we can no longer shop in the Occupied Territories. So our cost of living continues to rise because the exporters are greedy," she concludes.

Heavy import duties are also responsible for the high cost of living. "Here everything's more expensive. I've got a Volkswagen van which would cost about $12,000 in the States; here you can't buy it for anything less than $38,000," complains Bob Steinberger. "Basically the average salary here is about one third of the American wage, while the cost of living is about the same, only with higher taxes. How they afford those Volvos, Mercedes, BMWs, I don't know how they do it."

Given such constant complaining, it's understandable that the politicians come in for the bulk of the criticism. The paralysis of the Unity government evokes strong feelings from all parts of the political spectrum. "This country needs a governmental change, that is for sure. Change doesn't happen overnight, and nothing's going to happen in the next elections. We'll get the same gang of thieves in office," complains Ezra Gordesky.

"See that Laor poster showing Peres and Shamir pulling in opposite directions with Israel caught in the tug-of-war in the middle? That's how it is here. But it all goes to show that we're only a nation like any other. All they want to do is talk. Talk, talk, talk. Just like the Americans wish us to do. No, you've got to show strength, too. Look what we did with Lebanon and Syria. Do you think they want to attack us now?"

With nearly one third of its GNP spent on the military, Israel's continuing state of war with its neighbors and with its Palestinians has drained its economy for two generations now. "Just controlling things in the Occupied Territories during the intifada has cost the country over $600 million dollars — and a few hundred lives," notes Jerusalem accountant Miriam Mendes. "We can't afford that kind of drain and move ahead. So whether we like it or not, we've got to put aside all our other long-range plans and solve the Arab problem first."

Often lost in the hyperbole of daily complaints is the undeniable pride most Israelis exhibit in the country's undeniable success in the face of incredible odds. "This is a great country. Just a great country," beams the same Ezra Gordesky who only moments before had excoriated Israelis and their government. "We're willing to live on less because we see the benefits of a decent society. Despite the problems, we've got a wonderful little nation here, a place which comes closer to proper values." ■

*An Orthodox Jew and a Palestinian Arab. Can the one find peace with security in the same arrangement the other achieves it with dignity?*

*A Jew and an Arab intently reading their respective daily newspapers.*

198

*A member of the younger generation plays his hand-held computer game; an Iraqi studies Jewish mysticism in his Mea She'arim Sefardi temple.*

Greek Orthodox Priests meet on Good Friday outside
the Church of the Holy Sepulchre in Jerusalem.
OPPOSITE: Coptic priest, Jerusalem; Gush Emunim
leader, Rabbi Menachem Fruman of Tekoa; crucifer at
Palm Sunday service in the Old City; Samaritan elder
celebrates his version of Passover, complete with
slaughtering of sheep, atop Mt. Gerazim, near Nablus.

TWO ISRAELIS: THREE OPINIONS

*ABOVE: An off-duty soldier with his girlfriend;
a proud father with his young son during
Independence Day festivities, Jerusalem.
RIGHT: Three generations of Haredim.*

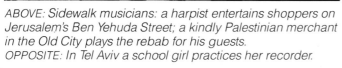

*ABOVE: Sidewalk musicians: a harpist entertains shoppers on Jerusalem's Ben Yehuda Street; a kindly Palestinian merchant in the Old City plays the rebab for his guests.*
*OPPOSITE: In Tel Aviv a school girl practices her recorder.*

*An Israeli cowboy from the Golan Heights.*

*A young Palestinian herdsman with his trusty steed.*

RIGHT: Winter training
for the IDF on the
slopes of Mt. Hermon
in the Golan Heights.
BELOW: Soldiers
patrol the beach in Tel
Aviv, stopping to chat
with some of their
peers; more serious
patrolling: laying
mines in training
exercises.

208

TOP LEFT: Reservist on Ben Yehuda Street; military duties are part of daily life and taken in stride by Israelis. In addition to their initial training and active duty, all men are required to serve 30-60 days reserve duty per year until age 55. Women serve for three years, but are not required to do reserve duty.

TOP RIGHT: Diversion while on routine guard duty atop the Old City walls.

LEFT: A member of the famed Golani Brigade on patrol in Ramallah on the West Bank. Many soldiers find guard duty in the Occupied Territories difficult due to conflicting emotions about the intifada and the resolution of the Palestinian question.

*Taunting Palestinian children; soldiers on patrol in Ramallah; smiling soldiers on patrol in an M-113 armored personel carrier near the Lebanese border.*

*How to be open when you're not open. This Palestinian green grocer has closed his shop to obey orders from the intifada organizers; he tries to continue a modicom of business on the sidewalk. Results of defying the intifada: fruit vendor's produce is smashed and left to rot in the streets of Jerusalem.*

211

*A construction worker stokes a fire to keep warm in late winter; a Druze fixes a truck tire in an Arab village outside the town of Daliyat el-Karmel.*

LEFT: A welder hard at work in Bet Yisra'el, Jerusalem. BELOW: A Palestinian shines shoes of tourists outside the Church of the Nativity in Bethlehem; a crescent is carefully re-attached to the Minbar (pulpit) on the platform of the Temple Mount, Jerusalem.

TWO ISRAELIS: THREE OPINIONS

*An Arab boy selling fresh bread outside the ancient Citadel. Arabs do the majority of the baking in Jerusalem; a Palestinian youth is engrossed in the simple pleasures of a spinning top in the streets of the Old City. OPPOSITE: An Arab youth contemplating a stone, with — perhaps — mixed emotions.*

ABOVE: Armenian schoolboy
studies English at the
Patriarchate's St. Tarkmanchatz
School in Jerusalem.
RIGHT: Pensive schoolgirl.
OPPOSITE: Son of a Gush
Emunim settler enjoys pizza in
Efrat; a future construction
worker plays in the sand; two
young Orthodox students
waiting for the bus; an Ethiopian
practices his basketball.

Ultra-Orthodox enjoy American baseball; song and dance characterize the spirit of celebration in Israel.
OPPOSITE: May Day parade in Tel Aviv, organized by the Histadrut Labour Federation.

# GLOSSARY

**Agudat Yisrael** Ultra-Orthodox religious party founded in 1912. Originally opposed to establishment of a secular state.

**Ahad Ha'am** (1856-1927) Russian-born Hassidic leader and philosopher who became the spiritual leader of cultural Zionism. Believed that a Jewish cultural renaissance in Palestine would strengthen life in the Diaspora, and that political Zionism was insufficient to resolve the Jewish problem.

**Alignment** Alliance of left-wing Mapam Party and Labour Party. Ruling coalition 1969-77.

**aliyah** Hebrew for ascent; used to denote immigration to Israel. Also used to denote specific waves of immigration. First Aliyah, 1881-1904; Second Aliyah, 1904-14; Third Aliyah 1919-23; Fourth Aliyah, 1924-8; Fifth Aliyah, 1929-39; Aliyah Bet (illegal immigrants), 1933-48. 1.8 million immigrated between 1948-86 in various aliyot (pl.) from numerous countries.

**Allon, Yigal** (1918-1980) Commander of the Palmach, 1945-8; commander of successful campaigns on all fronts in the War of Independence. Leading figure in Mapai, and served under Ben-Gurion and Eshkol as Minister of Labour.

**Ashkenazim** Jews of German or Eastern European origin, usually with Yiddish as an interlingua.

**Bar-Kochba, Shimon** (died 135 AD) Leader of bloody Judean revolt against Roman Emperor Hadrian, which resulted in the death of several hundred thousand Jews.

**Begin, Menachem** (1913 —) Russian-born rightwing underground leader of the IZL, and Prime Minister 1977-83. Begin was active in the Polish Betar Movement and organizing illegal immigration to Palestine. Came to Palestine in 1942, and after World War II led IZL against British authority. Led Herut in opposition to Mapai, and often had bitter clashes with Ben-Gurion. Formed Likud voting bloc, which won 1977 elections. Became Prime Minister and worked to achieve peace with Egypt. He and Anwar Sadat were awarded the Nobel Peace Prize in 1979.

**Ben-Gurion, David** (1886-1973) Polish-born Israeli statesman and first Prime Minister (1948-63); immigrated to Palestine in 1906. Forceful politician who built up IDF, while fighting dissident underground groups like the IZL and Lehi. Left government for two years, but returned to lead the country in the '56 Sinai Campaign. Resigned suddenly in 1963, and retired to Kibbutz Sde Boker in the Negev, from where continued to encourage desert settlement.

**Betar** Zionist youth movement originally affiliated with the Revisionist Movement; founded in 1923. Advocated immediate statehood, national military preparedness and service, and a code of honor. Became a recruiting source for militant undergrounds like IZL and Lehi, aided illegal immigration and helped lead revolts and sabotage against the Nazis in occupied Europe.

**Bnai Akiva** International Zionist Youth Movement; founded 1922.

**Chief Rabbinate** Originally established as the supreme religious authority in Palestine, now derives its authority from the secular government, a feature which has lead many ultra-Orthodox to object. Divides its authority between Ashkenazi and Sefardi representatives, and has ultimate decision powers in all matters religious. Conservative and Progressive (Reform) movements are excluded from the Chief Rabbinate.

**Dayan, Moshe** (1915-1981) Military general and political leader born in Kibbutz Degania. Served in the Haganah and the Palmach; became IDF Chief-of-Staff and led the successful Sinai Campaign in 1956. Minister of Defense, 1967-74. Became national hero after Six Day War, but lost much popularity and influence after Yom Kippur War in 1973. Foreign Minister under Menachem Begin, 1977-9.

**Deir Yassin** Former Arab village on western outskirts of Jerusalem where the IZL and Lehi massacred nearly 250 civilians in April, 1948. The murders were roundly condemned by the Jewish Agency, but spurred the departure of tens of thousands of Arabs from territory intended for inclusion in the State of Israel.

**Druze** A religious group which split from mainstream Islam in the 11th Century. About 70,000 Druze live in Israel in the Galilee and Mount Carmel regions; they enjoy full Israeli citizenship and serve in the IDF. About 580,000 live in Syria, 300,000 in Lebanon.

**Eban, Abba** (1915 —) South African-born diplomat and Member of Knesset. 1949-59 Eban was both Israel's representative to the United Nations and Ambassador to the United States. Long time Mapai member, Eban served, among other posts, as Minister of Foreign Affairs from 1966-74. Known as one of Israel's greatest orators.

**Eretz Yisrael** Hebrew for the Land of Israel.

**Eshkol, Levi** (1895-1969) Zionist Labour politician, Israel's second Prime Minister 1963-69, succeeding Ben-Gurion. Held many ministries, most importantly Finance (1952-63).

**Etzion Bloc** or Gush Etzion. A collection of West Bank settlements south of Jerusalem.

**Falasha** Common term for Ethiopian Jews, most of whom were brought to Israel in 1983-5 by the clandestine airlift "Operation Moses." Some Ethiopians resent the term "falasha" as derogatory. It is derived from the Amharic "group without land."

**Fedai'yin** Arabic for suicide squads; general term for terrorists who infiltrated to carry out terrorist acts before the 1967 War.

**Green Line** Armistice line between Israel and Arab neighbors from 1948-67. In Jerusalem the line ran just west of the Old City walls.

**Gur, Mordechai "Motta"** (1930 —) Labour Party politician and former Chief-of-Staff of the IDF (1974-8). Gur commanded the paratroopers who liberated Jerusalem in 1967. He was responsible for the Entebbe (Uganda) and Litani (Lebanon) Operations.

**Gush Emunim** Not a political party but an Orthodox spiritual movement that promotes settlement of Jewish villages in the occupied territories.

**Hadassah** Women's Zionist Organization of America, established in 1912 to instruct American women in Zionist principles. Fund raiser for medical and public health care in Palestine, Hadassah turned over all its health and welfare facilities to the Israeli government in 1960, retaining control of its two world-famous research hospitals in Jerusalem.

**Haganah** Hebrew word for "defense." Semi-underground Jewish defense forces in Palestine 1920-48; became Israeli Defense Forces.

**Halacha** Traditional Jewish religious law.

**Haredim** Ultra-Orthodox Jews who prefer the old European dress of the shtetls: black hat and long coat, sidecurls, beards. Many do not recognize the secular state at all.

**Hassidim** Followers of charismatic Jewish religious movement founded in 18th Century.

**Hebron** Judean city of 78,000 south of Jerusalem, and site of Abraham's Cave of the Patriarchs at Machpela. The environs include the massive West Bank settlement of Kiryat Arba, now a focal point of tension between Arab and Jew. Kiryat Arba people are led by the rightwing Gush Emunim Rabbi Moshe Levinger, and are perhaps the most outspoken of all in their advocacy of renewed Jewish presence in the West Bank.

**Herut** Right-wing party led by Menachem Begin; in 1973 took in smaller parties, including Simcha Erlich's Liberal Party to form Likud voting bloc.

**Herzl, Theodor** (1860-1904) Founder of political Zionism and World Zionist Organization. Herzl concluded that the only way to solve the anti-Semitic problem in Europe was for the Jews to emigrate to their own sovereign state.

**Histadrut** General Federation of Workers, founded 1920 and originally under virtual control of Mapai Party, although today it is non-political. Virtually a contradiction in terms, Histadrut combines a trade union, an economic employment system, a mutual aid society, a cultural activities center, a collection of sporting clubs. It includes Israel's second largest bank, the Bank Hapo'alim; the country's largest insurance company, Hasneh; and Israel's largest health fund, Kupat Holim. Histadrut's holding company, Hevrat Ha'ovdim, is the second largest employer in the country. About 1.5 million Israelis are members. The National Workers' Federation is a splinter group rival which rejects Socialist ideology.

**IDF (Israel Defense Forces)** Founded in 1948 as the logical outgrowth of the Haganah. Today the IDF is a combined-arms force with regular and reserve components in all branches. Under civilian control of the Ministry of Defense, the IDF Chief-of-Staff is invariably selected from the ranks of the army. Currently the IDF numbers about 450,000 men and women comprising 12 armored divisions and 20 infantry or paratroop brigades. The air force numbers some 80,000 persons, the navy about 20,000.

**Irgun Zva'i Le'umi (IZL)** Underground Jewish resistance organization founded in 1931 as military arm of Revisionist Movement. Conducted reprisal terrorist acts against Arabs in pre-State years; after World War II, under the leadership of Menachem Begin, the Irgun concentrated on anti-British activities. Its most infamous exploit was the dynamiting of the King David Hotel, where the British army was headquartered. The IZL was forcibly disbanded in 1948, many of its members were immediately enrolled into the IDF.

**Jabotinsky, Vladimir** (1880-1940) Russian-born Zionist leader of Revisionist Movement; philosophical mentor of Menachem Begin.

**Jewish Agency** During the Mandate, the Agency was originally the intermediary between the Yishuv and the British authorities, also the principal liaison between Eretz Yisrael and the Diaspora. Now synonymous with the World Zionist Organization.

**Jewish Brigade** Jewish volunteers who served in the British Army during World War II totalled 26,000. The Brigade of 5,000 was formed in 1944, and saw service in Egypt, Italy and Europe.

**Jewish Legion** Jewish military units (three battalions and the Zion Mule Corps, numbering about 6,400) raised to fight in British service during World War I and aid in the liberation of Palestine from Ottoman rule.

**Jewish National Fund** Founded in 1901 to purchase and develop land in Palestine for the WZO. The JNF purchased land on behalf of the Jewish people, and usually leased it for private use for a period of 49 years. By Independence more than a quarter million acres had been purchased by the JNF. After 1948 the JNF devoted most of its efforts to extensive afforestation and opening new areas for settlement.

**Kach** Rabbi Meir Kehane's party, established in 1971, and an outgrowth of his Jewish Defense League. An ultra rightwing minority party with a racist platform calling for the forced expulsion of Arabs from all Israel, the rejection of the Camp David Accords, the establishment of a reciprocal Jewish terrorist group, and other racist policies.

**Kafr Kassem** Israeli Arab village near Petach Tikva where 49 Arab villagers were killed by Border Police in 1956. Unaware of a curfew imposed on the eve of the Sinai Campaign, the men were shot when they returned from work. Eight police-

men were convicted and sentenced, to lengthy prison terms, although many were released early.

**Katznelson, Berl** (1887-1944) Ideologist of the Palestine labor movement, and a founder of Histadrut.

**Kehane, Meir** Brooklyn-born rabbi, founder of Jewish Defense League in USA and Kach Party in Israel. Immigrated to Israel in 1971. Elected to the 11th Knesset in 1984.

**kibbutz** (plural kibbutzim) Traditional Zionist-socialist agricultural settlement in Palestine, where all land, housing and means of production are owned by the cooperative. Members do not receive monetary reimbursement; all individual needs are provided by the cooperative. In recent decades many kibbutzim have also diversified into industrial production of specialized items.

**Knesset** Israel's 120-member unicameral parliament. Unlike other democracies where members are elected by constituencies, MKs are selected by a system of proportional representation from the lists of their various parties. The Knesset is elected for a period of four years, although it may be dissolved earlier and new elections set.

**Kollek, Teddy** (1911 —) Vienna-born Mayor of Jerusalem, 1965-present. Served as intelligence liaison with British and American intelligence services during World War II. Was Israel's minister in Washington 1951-2, and Director-General of Ben-Gurion's office 1951-64.

**Kook, Abraham Isaac** (1865-1935) First Ashkenazi Chief Rabbi of Palestine. Advocated strict Orthodoxy and Jewish nationalism as opposed to secular Zionist pioneers.

**Kook, Zvi Yehuda** (1891-1981) Son of Abraham Kook; became spiritual leader of Gush Emunim.

**Labour Party** Political party formed in 1968, amalgamating Mapai, Rafi and the Workers' Party, Ahdut Ha'avodah.

**Land Day** Arabs throughout Israel and the occupied territories "celebrate" March 30 as the anniversary of the day when Israeli army and police killed six persons protesting against government confiscation of land in the Galilee. The government position was that confiscation was required for further "regional development."

**Law of Return** 1950 Knesset law giving every Jew the right to immigrate to Israel. According to the Halacha, a "Jew" is any person who has converted or is born to a Jewish mother. Since then, a controversy has raged around the legitimacy of certain conversions. A 1952 law grants all such immigrants full citizenship if they so desire.

**Lehi** Otherwise known as the "Stern Gang" after founder Avraham Stern (1907-1942). Polish-born underground fighter. Broke with IZL in 1939 to form more militant Lehi. Believed in a Jewish state from the Nile to the Euphrates. Staunchly anti-

British, even to the extent of seeking relations with Fascist and Nazi regimes.

**Liberal Party** A centrist party allied with the Herut in the Likud bloc since 1965. Founded by the late Simcha Erlich, who advocated a private economy without government interference. Now the Liberals are headed by Yitzhak Moda'i, who wishes to merge his party within the Herut.

**Likud** Right-wing voting bloc established in 1973, combining Herut Party and other smaller groups under the leadership of Menachem Begin.

**Maki** The original Israel Communist Party. Arab members split off in 1965 to form Rakah Party.

**Mapai** Leading Labour Zionist Party, founded 1930. Was the ruling party under David Ben-Gurion; in 1968 became part of Labour Party. Formed Labour Alignment with Mapam in 1969, which held power until 1977.

**Mapam** Left-wing socialist party. Advocated militant socialism, Arab-Israeli accommodation.

**Meir, Golda** (1898-1978) Russian born, US raised Labour Party leader, Member of Knesset and Prime Minister, 1969-74. Made aliyah in 1921 and became active in Histadrut and Mapai. She resigned the Prime Ministership after the Agranat Report faulted governmental unpreparedness for the Yom Kippur War.

**moshav** (plural moshavim) Cooperative settlement based on private ownership of farmland and family dwellings, but with collective ownership and/or use of equipment.

**Mossad** Israel's foreign intelligence service.

**Nahal** Pioneering Fighting Youth; an outgrowth of Palmach principles and an alternative form of IDF military service where one splits his service time between kibbutz work and army training.

**National Religious Party (NRP)** Zionist religious party which strives to extend the law of the Torah into legislation while maintaining cooperation with all political elements.

**National Unity Government** Coalition governments in which both major political groups, Likud and Labour, are joined to achieve a majority in the Knesset because neither has a sufficient majority to govern. The present union dates from 1984, and required the Prime Minister's position to shift from Labour to Likud in 1986. New elections to be held in the fall of 1988.

**Oriental Jews** Another term for Sephardim, especially those of North African, Yemeni, Moroccan and Iraqi origin.

**Palestine Liberation Organization (PLO)** Established in 1964 as an organization lead by Yasser Arafat to represent the rights of Palestinian people, presumably Arabs, but not thusly defined in the Palestine National Covenant. Today

Arafat commands only a part of the PLO from his exile in Tunisia; many other groups have sprung up who refuse to recognize Arafat's control. Israel's official policy vis-a-vis the PLO is that it will not recognize an organization dedicated to terrorism, that refuses to accept the right of Israel to exist, and refuses to adhere to UN Resolutions 242 and 338. Currently there are about 700,000 Arab Israelis who live in the 1948 land, plus another 1.5 million who live in the West Bank and Gaza Strip.

**Palmach** Strike forces of the Haganah, 1941-48. First raised to provide protection against marauding Arabs, later in the front of the fighting against the British. Strong leftist-kibbutz and Mapam ties. Absorbed into the Haganah in 1948.

**Peace Now** Non-political peace movement founded in 1977. Seeks political accommodation with Israel's Arabs and neighboring Arab countries; opposes permanent settlements in the occupied territories. Stages large demonstrations to protest government policies it feels will impede peace between Jews and Arabs.

**Peres, Shimon** (1923 —) Polish-born Labour Party leader and former Prime Minister (1984-6). Peres has held many other cabinet posts, among them Minister of Defense (1975-7) and Minister of Foreign Affairs (1986-present). In recent decades, Peres has been a strong advocate of moderation and an increasing opponent of Likud Prime Minister Yitzhak Shamir's policies towards the occupied territories.

**protekzia** Colloquial term generally meaning influence, connections or "pull." What one is assumed to employ in order to make proper use of an advantage.

**Rabin, Yitzhak** (1922 —) Jerusalem-born military and political leader of Labour Party. Prime Minister 1974-7). He has held several cabinet posts, and was Ambassador to the United States; currently Rabin is Minister of Defense in the Unity government. From 1964-8 he was Chief-of-Staff of the IDF.

**Rakah** (New Communist List) Israel's Moscow-oriented, largely Arab Communist Party.

**Sabra and Shatilla** Palestinian refugee camps in Beirut where over 800 Palestinians were massacred by Lebanese Phalangist militia while they were ostensibly under the protection of IDF forces during Israel's invasion of Lebanon (Operation Peace for Galilee). Worldwide uproar resulted in Kahan Commission inquiry and censure for several military leaders; Defense Minister Ariel Sharon resigned as a result of the inquiry.

**Sephardim** Jews of Spanish origin, forced into second Diaspora in 1492; emigrated to countries in North Africa, southern Europe and Balkans. Ladino was original Sefardi interlingua.

**Shabak** Undercover group responsible for preventing espionage, terrorism and other hostile activity within the borders of Israel. Also known as the Shin Bet.

**Shamir, Yitzhak** (1915 —) Polish-born underground and Herut political leader. Twice Prime Minister (1983-4, 1986-8). In 1937 he joined the Irgun, later became a member of Lehi. In mid-'50s he was a ranking officer of the Mossad.

**Sharon, Ariel** (1928 —) Israel-born military leader and government minister. Nicknamed "Arik," Sharon has had a brilliant military career, first as a paratroop commander and then as an armored division commander in the 1967 War. He left the IDF for political life with the Likud, but was then recalled as a reserve general in the Yom Kippur War. Minister of Defense 1981-2, but forced to resign in the aftermath of the Sabra and Shatilla refugee camp massacres in Beirut. Currently he is Minister of Industry and Trade.

**Tehiya** Hebrew for revival. Right-wing nationalist party opposing West Bank autonomy, recognition of Palestinian civil rights, and many aspects of the Camp David Accords.

**Trumpeldor, Yosef** (1880-1920) Russian-born; Zionist pioneer and military leader. Helped raise Jewish Legion in the British Army, killed in 1920 defending Tel Hai in the northern Galilee against Arab attack. His dying words have become famous: "It is good to die for one's country," and were used as a continuing inspiration for the fighting Jews of the Revisionist Movement.

**Va'ad Le'umi** National Council of Palestine, elected by the Representative Assembly which functioned as the government of the Yishuv from 1920 to the establishment of the State in 1948.

**Wars of Israel** War of Independence 1948; Sinai Campaign 1956 (temporary occupation of Sinai while Britain and France invaded Suez); Six Day War 1967 (pre-emptive air strike against Egypt, Syria, Jordan, followed by occupation of West Bank, Gaza Strip and western parts of Golan Heights); War of Attrition 1968-70 (artillery duels across Suez Canal, anti-terrorist activities against PLO guerrillas operating primarily out of Egypt and Jordan); Yom Kippur War 1973 (following initial Egyptian and Syrian successes, supported by Iraq and Jordan, in invasion of Israel, IDF repelled its enemies and seized further parts of the Golan Heights from Syria); Lebanon 1982-3 (invasion of Lebanon north to Beirut in an attempt to permanently stamp out the PLO and its bases. It achieved only moderate success but great cost in materiel and world opinion).

**WASP** Not what you might think it is. In Israel an acronym for "White Ashkenazi Sabra with Protekzia," traditionally the socio-ethnic requirements for recognition in Israel, though much less so today with the successful integration of Sephardim into higher positions of authority.

**Weizman, Ezer** (1924 —) Israel-born air force general and cabinet minister; nephew of Israel's first President, Chaim Weizmann. Served in Royal Air Force in World War II, later in the IZL. Commanded the Israeli air force from 1958-66 and thoroughly modernized it; he received much of the credit for planning Israel's stunning victories over Arab air forces in '67 War when he was head of IDF General Staff Division. Joined Herut after leaving the military, and organized Menachem Begin's successful election campaign in 1977, serving as Minister of Defense from 1977-80. He was a major figure in securing Israeli participation in the Camp David Accords. In the last decade his political views have shifted away from the Herut, and he has become a leading proponent of peace with the Palestinians and Israel's Arab neighbors. Currently he is Minister Without Portfolio and in charge of running the Fall 1988 election campaign for the Labour Party.

**Weizmann, Chaim** (1874-1952) Russian-born professor of chemistry and First President of Israel. Weizmann was President of the Zionist Organization for much of the period 1920-48. Instrumental in promoting the Balfour Declaration and other important recognitions of the Zionist cause. An advocate of moderation in dealing with the British and the Arabs, Weizmann supported the partition of Palestine into separate states.

**White Paper** A British Mandatory policy statement of 1939 put a cap on further immigration beyond 75,000 additional Jews over five years, after which Palestine would be governed by an independent government with an Arab majority. In general, the Yishuv saw it as a surrender to Arab interests and a breach of faith. During World War II, Ben-Gurion advised the Yishuv to "fight the war as though there was no White Paper, and the White Paper as if there were no war."

**World Zionist Organization (WZO)** Founded by Theodor Herzl in 1897 to achieve the goals of Zionism. In 1929 established the Jewish Agency to act as an intermediary with the British Mandatory power. Following independence, the WZO and the Jewish Agency were continued, with the purpose of strengthening the State and aiding the ingathering. In recent decades the WZO has been a leading fund-raiser for Israel.

**Yahad** Hebrew for "together." Ezer Weizman's 1984 political creation, hoping to gather in former military leaders and business people who had no previous political connections. Advocates flexibility towards Arabs. Yahad joined the unity Government to forestall a Likud majority.

**Yammit** Israeli settlement in Sinai forcibly evacuated and then bulldozed by IDF forces in 1982 to satisfy terms of peace treaty with Egypt. The incident has become a rallying point for right-wingers who do not wish to trade territories for peace with the Palestinians.

**Yeshivot Hesder** Jewish religious academies where students combine religious studies with military service. As the Knesset is considering revocation of the military exemption for religious scholars, the Yeshivot Hesder are expected to grow far beyond their 5,000 man strength.

**Yishuv** Hebrew for community. General term for the Jewish community in pre-state Palestine.

# PHOTOGRAPHY